D1008854

THE CASE FOR
TRANSRACIAL ADOPTION

THE CASE FOR TRANSRACIAL ADOPTION

Rita J. Simon
Howard Altstein
Marygold S. Melli

THE AMERICAN UNIVERSITY PRESS

Copyright © 1994 by
The American University Press
4400 Massachusetts Avenue, N.W.
Washington, D.C. 20016

Distributed by arrangement with
University Publishing Associates℠
4720 Boston Way
Lanham, MD 20706

3 Henrietta Street
London WC2E 8LU England

Library of Congress Cataloging-in-Publication Data

Simon, Rita James.
The case for transracial adoption / Rita J. Simon, Howard
Altstein, Marygold S. Melli.
p.   cm.
Includes bibliographical references and index.
1. Interracial adoption—United States.   2. Intercountry
adoption—United States.   3. Adoption.   I. Altstein, Howard.
II. Melli, Marygold Shire.   III. Title.
HV875.64.S5574   1993
362.7'34'0973—dc20   93–20749 CIP

ISBN 1–879383–19–5 (cloth : alk. paper)
ISBN 1–879383–20–9 (pbk. : alk. paper)

 The paper used in this publication meets the minimum requirements of
American National Standard for Information Sciences—Permanence
of Paper for Printed Library Materials, ANSI Z39.48–1984.

Contents

Tables

Acknowledgments

More than 20 years have gone by since we began much of the work described in this volume. Throughout this time we have had extraordinary support and cooperation from the families (parents and children) who formed our study group. We appreciate their help and recognize that without it we could not have carried on for more than two decades. We also want to express thanks to our field staff, most of whom were graduate students in 1971, 1979, 1983, and 1990 at the universities of Illinois, Minnesota, and Michigan, Washington University in St. Louis, and The American University in Washington, D.C. They conducted interviews that lasted from 40 minutes to two hours, in the respondents' homes. Finally, we acknowledge our appreciation to Joyce Turner, Frances Norwood, and Linda Ireland for their excellent clerical help. They all demonstrated diligence, patience, and efficiency in processing this manuscript from draft stage to final form.

1

Transracial and Intercountry Adoptions: How Many and from Which Countries

Transracial adoption (TRA) and intercountry adoption (ICA) began in the late 1940s following the end of a world war that left thousands of children homeless in many parts of the world. The incidence of such adoptions gained momentum in the mid-1950s, diminished during the early 1960s, rose again in the late 1960s, and began to decline in the mid-1970s. From a high of more than 2,500 transracial adoptions reported in 1971, less than 1,000 were made in 1975.

Transracial adoption did not come about as a result of deliberate agency programming to serve populations in need; rather, it was an accommodation to reality. Social changes in the United States—changes regarding abortion, contraception, and reproduction in general—significantly reduced the number of white children available for adoption, leaving nonwhite children as the largest available source. Changes had also occurred regarding the willingness of white couples to adopt nonwhite children. Whatever the reasons, in order to remain "in business," adoption agencies were forced by a combination of social conditions to reevaluate their ideology, traditionally geared toward the matching concept, in order to serve the joint needs of parentless children and couples seeking to adopt.

How Many Children Are Involved

Presenting accurate, reliable, and meaningful data about transracial and intercountry adoptions is not an easy task. In some cases, numbers are unavailable for political reasons. Their revelation might constitute an embarrassment either to a particular country or to a specific child welfare agency. Countries may not be anxious to advertise the actual numbers of children they allow to leave their shores for adoption in (more affluent, white) Western countries. Neither may they want the world to know how many children are living in orphanages, many times under highly questionable conditions. Concerning transracial adoptions within the United States, agencies may not want to reveal that a larger than expected percentage of nonwhite children remain for long periods of time in foster care, group homes, or institutions.

There are also instances in which numbers are unavailable because they have not been collected. But in all of the above scenarios, the results are similar. Policymakers, researchers, and the public are deprived of valuable information, which, if available, could be used to formulate practical social policies that might alleviate the persistent problem of parentless children.

This chapter presents what numbers *are* available for transracial and intercountry adoptions, and an account of the practices that helped create those figures. In addition, the chapter discusses issues we believe are related to adoption: birthrates, abortion, teenage pregnancies, and a lessening stigma on unwed motherhood.

Transracial Adoptions

At the time of writing, the United States had not been collecting data since 1975 on the number of in-racial and transracial adoptions that occur per year, the number of children available for adoption, or the number of children in foster care; and even before 1975, the numbers were often incomplete. Since 1980, the U.S. government has failed to implement its own law as it was spelled out in P.L. 96-272—the Adoption Assistance and Child Welfare Act of 1980—which mandated the creation of "a statewide information system capable of tracking children . . . who had received care within the preceding twelve months."

Under President Ronald Reagan, this provision of the statute was interpreted as being voluntary on the part of the states. In 1986, another statute was enacted that also called for the implementation of an information system that would account for the number of children in foster care and for those who were adopted. The law provided that this system should be operational by October 1991. Just prior to its implementation, a commissioner of the Health and Human Services Department (HHS) wrote that regulations were still being written and that states were not required to submit any data until such time as the regulations are finalized.

As recently as November 1991, in a call made to HHS by one of the authors, we were told that the federal government did not know when the 1986 (actually, the 1980) statute would be implemented. No reason was given as to why. All of us are thus without any reliable and consistent sources of data; it is up to researchers to ferret out information from various reports, articles, records, and so forth, and then—based on their knowledge of the field—make some educated projections about the number of children involved.

Black American Children

We do know that, compared to in-racial adoptions, transracial adoptions have always involved only a small number of parentless black children. For example, from 1968 to 1975, approximately 12,000 black children were placed with white families. The year 1971 saw the greatest number of black children transracially adopted: 2,574. In the government's most recent report on adoptions, which appeared in 1975 and was based on data from only 23 states, the Government Accounting Office (GAO) stated that approximately 2 percent of all adoptions "involved black children placed with parents who were not black."

Although the government stopped collecting data on adoptions in 1975, other groups have tried to fill the gap. Four sources of information are the Child Welfare League of America (CWLA), the National Center for Health Statistics (NCHS), the National Committee for Adoption (NCFA), and the North American Council on Adoptable Children (NACAC). In a 1990 report based on a 1987 survey, the NCHS stated that "interracial adoptions, which constituted about 8 percent of all adoptions . . . , consisted primarily of the adoption of children of races other than black or white by white adoptive mothers."[1] Elsewhere in the same issue, the 8-percent figure was more closely examined: "Five percent were adoptions of children of races other than white or black by white mothers, 1 percent were adoptions of black children by white mothers, and 2 percent were adoptions of white children by mothers of other races."[2]

Thus, in 1987, traditional patterns of transracial adoption (black children placed with white families) accounted for no more than 1 percent of all U.S. adoptions. In the NCHS report, next to the figure for the category *white mother, black child,* there was an asterisk indicating, "Figure does not meet standard of reliability or precision."[3]

In 1989, the CWLA issued a report entitled *The State of Adoption in America.* The report was based on a survey conducted in 1988 of 48 public agencies in the 50 U.S. states plus the District of Columbia, Puerto Rico, and the Virgin Islands. Of the 53 questionnaires that were sent out, 48 were completed and returned. In addition, 138 private agencies were also surveyed, from which 103 questionnaires were completed and returned.

The figures in Table 1.1 describe the results of the public agencies surveyed. The data show that the 48 public child welfare agencies were responsible for 25,175 children awaiting adoption. The authors report

On the average, these children have been "waiting" for 632 days, or almost two years. Approximately 80 percent of these children are seen as having "special needs" concerning adoptive placement, in that they are older, severely handicapped, or are members of sibling groups. Around 51 percent of the children "waiting" are members of minority groups.[4]

Seven of the 48 agencies did not report the number of parents or children waiting. Of the 41 that did, 16 showed more parents than children waiting. The states that showed the greatest disparity between children available and parents waiting were California, Connecticut, Florida, Georgia, Illinois, Michigan, Minnesota, Mississippi, Missouri, Nevada, New York, Oklahoma, and South Carolina. Of the 13 states listed above, Florida, Illinois, Michigan, Minnesota, and New York reported many more children waiting than there were parents available.

Thirteen of the 38 states for which data are filled in for each column show that more than 50 percent of the children waiting are of minority racial background.

When respondents were asked which factors were most important in preventing the public agencies from arranging adoptions, the answers most often given were: (1) the number of minority children and of children with special needs awaiting adoption, which exceeded the number of minority and other families recruited to adopt them; (2) the time it took to terminate legally the birth parents' rights; and (3) the agencies' lack of staff and resources. For example, J. Mason and C. W. Williams reported that in 1982 there were 16,235 black children who were free for adoption. Adoptive placements had been found for about 4,000, or 25 percent, of them.[5] They also reported that the percentage of black children who remained in foster care for more than four years was 34.6 percent, compared to 17.7 percent for white children. Mason and Williams also pointed out that, when family composition, income, and age were controlled, the 1982 rate of adoption was 18 black children per 10,000 black families, compared to four white children per 10,000 families. These data confirm a statistic long known to adoption professionals: that black families adopt at a higher rate than white families.

The results of the survey conducted of private agencies showed that in 1987 those agencies handled 4,822 adoptions, about one-third of which were intercountry adoptions. Of the domestic adoptions, more than 90 percent were by persons not related to the child, and 75 percent of those adoptions were of infants less than one year of age. The majority of the infants were white and healthy.

The report stated that "84 percent of the responding public and private agencies say they have a waiting list of adoptive parent applicants." Looking only at the public agencies, the report stated that "for each child waiting for adoption, there are 1.2 adoptive parent applicants. For the private agencies, there are 1.8 adoptive parent applicants for each available child."[6]

In 1991, the North American Council on Adoptable Children (NACAC) released a report entitled, "Barriers to Same Race Placement."[7] The report is based on a survey conducted in 1990 of minority adoptions, both in-racial and transracial. The report reflected 1989–90 figures and was based on responses from 87 adoption agencies in 25 states. The total number of children in the survey was 13,208, of whom 6,542 were nonwhite (black, Hispanic, Native American, and other).

The report stated that almost 78 percent of all the black children in the survey were placed with black families. But when adoption agencies were divided into "minority placement specialists" and "traditional nonspecializing agencies," different relationships were uncovered relevant to TRA. For example, those agencies that fell into the category of minority placement specialists in-racially placed 94 percent of their black children, while traditional nonspecializing agencies placed only 51 percent of their black children with black families. Thus, 49 percent of the black children under the authority of traditional nonspecializing agencies were transracially placed (eight of these agencies transracially placed 85 percent of their nonwhite children), as compared with only 6 percent of those assigned to minority placement specialists. Additionally, about two-thirds of the adoptable black children in Southern-state traditional nonspecializing agencies were trans-

Table 1.1   State Child Welfare Agency Reports on Children and Adults Waiting for Adoptions, 1988

State	Number of Children Waiting[1]	Percent Minority[2]	Percent Special Needs[3]	Number of Parents Waiting[4]
Alabama	259	51	87	263
Arizona	125	43	95	0
Arkansas	279	30	80	60
California	628	83	86	1,467
Colorado	40	25	100	80
Connecticut	203	58	65	3,000
Delaware	14	57	100	0
District of Columbia	53	100	100	24
Florida	1,200	35	100	200
Georgia	443	60	92	2,000
Hawaii	206	NA	90	28
Idaho	18	2	70	39
Illinois	2,600	48	70	1,183
Indiana	426	33	90	152
Iowa	90	1	95	160
Kansas	243	17	90	138
Louisiana	670	54	25	NA
Maine	50	0	100	135
Massachusetts	1,757	33	70	NA
Michigan	1,388	49	90	0
Minnesota	667	12	75	0
Mississippi	125	70	90	1,000
Missouri	419	41	91	1,049
Montana	80	10	100	0
Nebraska	82	13	100	0
Nevada	67	47	100	1,200
New Hampshire	29	7	100	20
New Jersey	1,850	85	100	NA
New Mexico	504	60	85	250
New York	2,727	71	NA	1,000
North Carolina	395	48	72	NA
North Dakota	7	0	100	433
Ohio	1,500	60	90	NA
Oklahoma	338	30	86	900
Oregon	250	10	90	150
Pennsylvania	1,663	NA	NA	NA

(cont'd)

Table 1.1, continued

State	Number of Children Waiting[1]	Percent Minority[2]	Percent Special Needs[3]	Number of Parents Waiting[4]
Puerto Rico	466	100	4	224
Rhode Island	75	32	99	90
South Carolina	636	65	72	1,535
South Dakota	34	70	100	60
Tennessee	605	33	82	612
Texas	768	40	70	200
Vermont	9	10	100	49
Virginia	368	56	74	310
Washington	559	10	NA	200
West Virginia	NA	NA	NA	148
Wisconsin	257	32	100	135
Wyoming	3	0	100	0

Notes: Telephone conversations with state agency respondents make clear that some of the figures are estimates rather than exact records. Furthermore, because states use different definitions and means of reporting, the numbers above cannot be easily compared from one state to another. They do instead indicate overall patterns. "NA" means not available.

1. Agency responses to this question: "How many children under the care and responsibility of your agency are considered to be 'waiting' for adoption according to your state policy either formal or informal or practice?"

2. Agency responses to this question: "What percentage of the children are minority?"

3. Agency responses to this question: "What percentage of the children waiting have 'special needs'?"

4. Agencies were asked, "Does your agency have a waiting list for adoptive parent applicants?" and "If yes, how many applicants are on this list?" The numbers above are for state agencies stating they do have such a waiting list; agencies stating they do not have such a list show "0" in this column.

Source: Joyce Matthews Munns and Jacquelyn A. Copenhaven, *The State of Adoption in America,* report of the Child Welfare League of America, New York, 1989.

racially adopted, as compared with less than half of available black children in other regions of the country assigned to similar agencies.

To a large extent, the National Committee for Adoption (NCFA) has filled the vacuum left when the federal government stopped collecting and disseminating national adoption figures. NCFA conducts its own surveys and publishes a useful sourcebook called the *Adoption Factbook.*[8] NCFA figures are cited by the U.S. Bureau of the Census in their publications relevant to adoption. In neither the 1989 or 1991 editions of the *Adoption Factbook* are there figures for transracial adoptees. In a December 2, 1991, telephone conversation, the president of NCFA, Dr. William Pierce, stated that there are "no new TRA data."

Native American Children

Relatively large proportions of Native American children have been adopted transracially. In 1968, Native American minors constituted 7 percent of the population, but accounted for 70 percent of all adoptions in South Dakota. In 1969, a 16-state report indicated that about 89 percent of all Native American children in foster care were placed transracially. In 1972, one of four Native American children under one year of age was adopted in Minnesota. In 1974, up to 35 percent of all Native American children were removed from their families and placed in foster care, institutionalized, or adopted. By 1978, Minnesota reported that 90 percent of all nonrelated Native American adoptions were transracial. During the same period, in Wisconsin, the likelihood of Native American children being removed from their families was 1,600 percent greater than that for non–Native Americans. In Washington State, Native Americans constituted less than 2 percent of the population, but accounted for 19 percent of the adoptions. Only 19 of 119 Native American children were adopted by Native American families. The remaining 100 were adopted transracially. A 1978 study found that Native American children constituted 2 percent of all children legally free for adoption in the United States, or approximately 2,040 children. Overall, the rate at which Native American children were being adopted was 20 times higher than the national rate.

The Indian Child Welfare Act of 1978 (P.L. 95-608)—cited in Chapter 2—was designed to prevent the decimation of Indian tribes and the breakdown of Indian families by transracial placement of Native American children. The law makes it almost impossible for non–Native American couples to adopt Native American children or receive them in foster placement. P.L. 95-608 was intended to safeguard Native American culture by keeping families and tribes together and within their native environments.

Intercountry Adoptions to the United States

Intercountry adoptions of European orphans by American families began when World War II ended. One of the provisions of the Displaced Persons Act of 1948 pertained to "orphan immigrants" as a special category of refugee. Under the 1948 act, 4,065 such orphans entered the United States. Under the Refugee Acts of 1953, some 1,800 additional orphaned children gained entry.

During this same period—1948–53—2,418 Asian-born children were brought to the United States as a result of intercountry adoptions, two-thirds (1,602) of whom were Japanese.

The second phase of ICA—and the one that now appears to be slowly waning—began in the mid-1950s, again as a Western response to children made parentless by an international conflict. This time it was the Korean War, and the children involved were Korean. The adoption of these children by Westerners presaged an era in child placement that was different from the largely similar children (racially and culturally speaking) adopted as a result of World War II. For the first time in history, relatively large numbers of Western couples—mostly in the United States—were adopting children racially and culturally different from themselves.

Between 1953 and 1962, approximately 15,000 foreign-born children were adopted by American families. From 1963 to 1976, approximately 32,000 additional foreign-born children were adopted by U.S. citizens. About 65 percent of these children came from Asia, and the largest group from a single country were born in the Republic of Korea.

During the period 1963–76, of the Western European children adopted by Americans, some 60 percent were born in West Germany or Italy. It is interesting to note that, while Western European families adopted many non-European-born children, West Germany continued to "export" orphans until as recently as 1981. From 1976 to 1981, there were 304 West German–born children adopted by Americans. One explanation is that many of these children were racially mixed—the offspring of black U.S. servicemen stationed in Germany. These children might have had a difficult time being fully accepted into mainstream German society.

Between 1977 and 1987, there were 77,908 foreign-born children adopted by American couples. In the four-year span from 1984 to 1987, about 60 percent of the almost 38,000 foreign-born children adopted by American families came from Korea. In 1987 alone, 10,097 foreign-born children were adopted in the United States. That figure is 50 percent higher than it was 1974. The rate of increased ICAs into the United States appears to be matched by the Western European experience. It is estimated that about 10,000 intercountry adoptees enter Western Europe each year. This figure approximates 1 percent of all European "new births."

But recent developments within the Republic of Korea and other countries that have sanctioned the almost unrestricted adoption of their children by Westerners indicate that this practice may soon be changed, with the result that the number of children available for adoption will be greatly reduced. For example, an editorial that appeared in the *Korean Herald* in November 1990 stated, "Being labeled as a major exporter of orphans is definitely a shame for any country. The time has come for the nation to wipe out the disgrace."[9]

Korea is not the only country reducing the number of children it allows to leave for adoption purposes. Some Latin American countries—such as Paraguay, Ecuador, and Brazil—are also curtailing the number of intercountry adoptions they will allow. In most cases, the reasons given by countries for their decision to curb this practice are "irregularities." The latter are usually defined as the selling of children. A less explicitly stated reason is one based on nationalistic resentment against the practice of allowing their children to be adopted by Westerners.

One bright spot for adopters has been Colombia, which has allowed a comparatively large number of its children to leave the country for adoption by Western families. For the past several years, it has allowed about 3,800 children to be placed with Western families each year. Taiwan, Thailand, Poland, Hong Kong, Mexico, and Central America all continue to increase marginally the number of children they allow to be adopted in the West. The overall numbers, however, are not large.

Cost of Adoption

A discussion of the costs involved in transracial and intercountry adoption is presented because we feel it affects not only how many children are adopted, but who adopts them. An argument made by some opponents of either transracial adoption or intercountry adoption is that adoption is a social class exchange in which the rich and privileged possess the means to buy the children of the poor and disadvantaged.

With respect to TRA, the National Association of Black Social Workers (NABSW) contends that the costs involved in adoption serve as a barrier to increasing the number of black families that agencies deem eligible to adopt, and thereby increase the likelihood of TRA. Usually more affluent white families have the resources to satisfy the "means test" criteria established by agencies for status as an adoptive parent, and are better able to absorb the legal fees associated with an adoption.

It is somewhat difficult to discuss the exact costs involved in adopting a foreign-born child since there is no central repository collecting these figures. But in several parent support newsletters that discuss these matters, there appears to be a consensus on the costs involved, plus or minus a few thousand dollars. One newsletter reported that from 1986 to 1990, the cost of an intercountry adoption rose approximately 40 percent, with the average Asian adoption costing about $10,000. Intercountry adoption from Latin America averaged $14,000; but it was becoming increasingly common to pay $20,000, and in some cases more. Another newsletter reported that in 1989 the average cost for an intercountry adoption was $10,200, with a range of from $7,000 to $15,000. On the average, families had to wait 13 months for their adoptees from the time of initial application. The figure $17,000 was also reported—in 1991, for intercountry adoptions from Peru, Chile, and Brazil. In November 1991, *Time* magazine reported that the costs of intercountry adoptions ranged from $5,000 to $20,000.[10]

In speaking with adopters, potential adopters, and agency personnel, we heard a possible explanation for why Latin American adoptions cost more than Asian adoptions do. The reason rests on the cultural and racial preferences of the adopters, namely, that there is a greater likelihood of adopting a Caucasian or Caucasian-appearing child from Latin America than from Asia. Along the same lines, in 1990 a U.S. agency published the following fees involved in adopting a U.S.-born child from its agency:

White infants	$7,500.00
Biracial infants	$3,800.00
Black infants	$2,200.90

It appears that an agency can demand and receive greater fees for white or biracial infants than it can for black infants, because the former are scarcer.

Factors Contributing to Fewer Adoptable Children

Four factors seem to affect directly the numbers of native-born children available for adoption in the United States, which in turn influence the rates of transracial and intercountry adoptions. Those factors are a *declining birthrate*, a *steady rate of infertility*, the *availability of abortions*, and a *changed social attitude toward unwed mothers* who choose to parent their children.

Reduced Stigma on Unwed Mothers

Change in attitudes toward unwed motherhood may have been a contributing factor in explaining why only 2 percent of all single mothers in the United States chose to place their infants for adoption between 1982 and 1988. That 2-percent surrender figure, alone, partially explains the sharp reduction in the number of adoptable infants in the United States. But this minimal surrender percentage takes on added significance for several reasons. Birthrates of unwed mothers have steadily risen to the point where almost 25 percent (23.3 percent) of all births for the period July 1989–June 1990 were to unmarried women. During this same one-year period, more than two-thirds of all teenagers who gave birth were unmarried. The period 1987–89 saw a 19-percent increase in birthrates for females between 15 and 17 years of age. In fact, in the five-year period ending in 1989, the overwhelming majority (81 percent) of women aged 15–17 who were having children were unwed. The figure for unwed mothers aged 18–19 was slightly less (59 percent).

These figures are important because historically it was from the cohort of unwed mothers, and especially teenagers, that the pool of adoptable children was established. The more out-of-wedlock births there were, the larger the pool of adoptable children. But in the 1990s, the stigma of unwed motherhood has been reduced considerably, making it easier for unwed mothers to parent their child(ren) in familylike environments. Another reason women may no longer be so

Table 1.2   Percentage of Births to Unwed Females, by Race, July 1989–June 1990

Race of Unwed Mother	Percent Unwed
White	17.2
Black	56.7
Hispanic	23.2
All mothers	23.3

Source: Compiled by the authors.

Table 1.3   Percentage of Births to Unwed Females, by Age and Year

	Percent Unwed		
Age	*1965–69*	*1975–79*	*1985–89*
15–17	41	59	81
18–19	20[1]	37[2]	59

Notes:
1. Late 1960s.
2. Late 1970s.
Source: Compiled by the authors.

likely to place their children for adoption is the availability of child care, which allows the single mother to work outside the home, knowing that her child is receiving adequate supervision. Whatever the reasons, we can clearly make two related statements: more unwed women are having children, and more are keeping them; and these facts influence the number of adoptable infants in the United States.

Infertility and Birthrate

In 1988, about 8.4 percent of all women between the ages of 15 and 44 experienced "an impaired ability to have children." The percent was 25 percent for women in their mid-thirties. As important as the 25-percent figure—because it is between the ages of 35 and 44 that the "adoption option" becomes so significant—is the fact that, from 1982 to 1988, the percentage of women in this age bracket with impaired fecundity rose to 37 percent.

Abortion

By 1989 the abortion rate for U.S. women was 1.9 percent higher than in 1988, for a total of 1.4 million known abortions. But the ratio of abortions to live births diminished somewhat, from 352 in 1988 to 346 per 1,000 in 1989. It is difficult to compare national abortion figures with individual state figures because many times states do not require hospitals and clinics to report their data.

Once again, the relevance of abortion rates rests on the assumption that these rates inversely influence the number of infants available for adoption. In other words, if one accepts that there is, or might be, a connection between abortion rates and the number of children available for adoption, then the number of children placed for adoption should decrease as the number of abortions rises. Some data do exist that—if one is inclined to define the inverse relationship between abortion and adoption as reasonable—could be used to support this hypothesis. For example, prior to *Roe v. Wade* (1973) there were about 95,000 adoptions per year in the United States.[11] Since *Roe v. Wade*, the number of adoptions has fallen to approximately 50,000. Clearly, however, it would be a simplistic interpretation to conclude that no other events occurred to explain the differences in adoption rates.

The major message that emerges from the data in this chapter is the need for accurate and reliable information on the number and characteristics of children available for adoption, the settings in which they are awaiting adoption, the number and types of families ready to adopt, and the number and types of adoptions that occur each year.

Notes

1. "Adoption in the 1980s," National Center for Health Statistics, Washington, D.C., 1990, p. 1.
2. Ibid., p. 6.
3. Ibid., p. 10.
4. Joyce Matthews Munns and Jacquelyn A. Copenhaven, *The State of Adoption in America,* report of the Child Welfare League of America, New York, 1989.
5. J. Mason and C. W. Williams, "The Adoption of Minority Children: Issues in Developing Law and Policy," in *Adoption of Children with Special Needs: Issues in Law and Policy* (Washington, D.C.: American Bar Association, 1985), p. 83.
6. Munns and Copenhaven, *State of Adoption*, p. 8.
7. "Barriers to Same Race Placement," report of the North American Council on Adoptable Children, St. Paul, Minn., 1991.
8. *Adoption Factbook,* sourcebook of the National Committee for Adoption, Washington, D.C., various years.
9. Editorial, *Korean Herald*, November 1990, p. 6.
10. *Time* (October 21, 1991), p. 87.
11. *Roe v. Wade*, 410 U.S. 113 (1973).

2

The Law Governing
Transracial Adoptions

This chapter describes the two quite different legal settings in which transracial adoptions take place. One is the domestic adoption arena in which children who are U.S. residents are selected and placed for adoption, usually in the state in which they reside. The other is the more complex world of intercountry adoptions, involving bureaucracies at the state, federal, and foreign levels. The first part of this chapter examines the state legal setting for domestic transracial adoptions. The second part describes the intercountry situation.

Adoption Laws in the 50 States

Transracial adoptions are governed by the same laws as other adoptions. Adoption, like other family law issues, is the province of the states; and therefore, the law of the state in which the adoption is to take place will control the arrangements. Transracial adoptions are similar to other adoptions except for the role that race may play in the adoption process. Therefore, this discussion of state adoption law focuses on the issue of race in adoption decisions. It explores the issue of why, in a society committed to racial color blindness and where the law requires that racial classifications be strictly scrutinized, black children can be denied suitable homes because the available adoptive parents are white.

The legal structure for adoption consists of the adoption statutes, case law interpreting those statutes, and—perhaps most important—the placement practices of the public and private adoption agencies whose role it is, first, to provide services to parents who wish to place children for adoption and, second, to choose adoptive homes in which those children will be placed.

This legal structure shares the common objective of seeking adoptions that are in the best interest of the child. For much of the history of adoption in the United States, adoption professionals have seen the best interest of the child as being promoted by a policy of matching children and adoptive parents. The Fifth Circuit Court of Appeals has described the process as follows:

> [Adoption agencies] try to place a child where he can most easily become a normal family member. The duplication of his natural biological environment is a part of that program. Such factors as age, hair color, eye color and facial features of parents and child are considered in reaching a decision. This flows from the belief that a child and adoptive parents can best adjust to a normal family relationship if the child is placed with adoptive parents who could have actually parented him. To permit consideration of physical characteristics necessarily carries with it permission to consider racial characteristics.[1]

This matching policy has resulted in a unique body of law that allows far greater consideration of racial background than is normally tolerated under the constitutional law of the United States.[2]

Statutory Framework

Race in State Statutes

Each state has a set of statutes regulating the placement and adoption of children. These statutes specify that the objective of the adoption law is to serve the best interest of the child. The majority of these statutory statements do not mention race in connection with the adoption process. However, a substantial minority—approximately 20 jurisdictions—do refer explicitly to race in their adoption laws. Ten of these jurisdictions[3] simply provide that the race of one or more of the parties directly affected by the adoption is to be included in the petition for adoption or listed as a finding in a court-ordered or statute-mandated investigation. The statutes are silent as to how this information should be used by those in a position to make final decisions concerning adoption; but, given the underlying public policy, it follows that they are part of a process that definitely takes race into consideration.

Seven states—Kentucky, Maryland, New Jersey, Connecticut, Pennsylvania, Texas, and Wisconsin—have statutory provisions that are much more in the mainstream of U.S. constitutional law dealing with race: they prohibit the use of race to deny an adoption or placement. Three of these states—Wisconsin, Texas, and Pennsylvania—prohibit discrimination on the basis of race in adoption, without qualification. Texas, in legislation effective May 1993, explicitly provides that a court may not delay or deny an adoption and an agency may not delay or deny a placement for adoption on the basis of race. Wisconsin states that no qualified applicant may be denied the benefits of the adoption statute on the basis of race; Pennsylvania provides that the racial background of the adopting parents or child shall not preclude an adoption. Two more states—Connecticut and Maryland—specify that an adoption cannot be denied solely on the basis of race. The other two statutes qualify their prohibitions. The New Jersey statute, for example, provides that an agency may not discriminate with regard to the selection of adoptive parents on the basis of race, but then provides that race may be considered in determining the best interest of the child. Somewhat similarly, agencies in Kentucky may not deny placement on the basis of race, unless the biological parents have expressed a clear desire to so discriminate, in which case their wishes must be respected.

In contrast to the silence of most state laws and the admonition of a few that race ought not to interfere with an adoption, and contrary to the accepted treatment of race elsewhere in the law, three states— Arkansas, California, and Minnesota—have laws that specifically require preference to be given to adoption within the same racial group.[4] In all three jurisdictions, the first preference is for a blood relative, the second for a family of the same race as the child, and the last for placement with a family "knowledgeable and appreciative of the child's racial or ethnic heritage."[5] The Arkansas statute limits this hierarchical approach to adoption placements involving "minority children," but the other two states require the racial and ethnic matching for all adoptive children. These statutes appear to be a response to the policy advocating that black children should be adopted only by black parents, as discussed in detail in Chapter 3.

Of these three statutes, the Arkansas statute requiring racial matching for minority children only would appear to be facially unconstitutional. In fact, a Minnesota Court of Appeals has held a similarly restricted Minnesota statute to be unconstitutional. In *Matter of Welfare of D. L.*,[6] a white couple who had petitioned to adopt the two-year-old black child placed with them when she was four days old brought the challenge against the Minnesota statute as a violation of the equal protection clause. The maternal grandparents had also petitioned to adopt, and the trial court had considered the grandparents' petition first—reasoning that, under the statute, only if it found good cause not to follow the statutory family preference would it need to reach other issues. After a trial on the issue of whether there was good cause not to grant the grandparents' petition, the trial court granted it. The court of appeals held the statute to be unconstitutional, but affirmed the trial court grant of adoption on the basis of a preference for adoption within the family. It found that the statute established a racial classification requiring the trial court to follow certain preferences for minority children, not required for nonminority ones. The racial classification failed, it said, because it was not necessary to accomplishing the legislative purpose. A racially neutral statute— applying to all children—would accomplish the same result. (The Minnesota statute was amended in 1992 to require racial matching for all children, not just minority children.)

On appeal, the Minnesota Supreme Court did not reach the issue of whether the statute was constitutional, because it found that the best interest of the child was promoted by the statutory preference for family placement. It pointed out that adoption petitions are to be granted if doing so is in the best interest of the child.

> In the courts' efforts to identify and promote the best interests of children, we have repeatedly noted our strong preference for permanent placement of children with relatives. . . . Accordingly, we hold today that adoptive placement with a family member is presumptively in the best interests of the child, absent a showing of good cause to the contrary or detriment to the child.[7]

The present Minnesota statute and the California statutes—unlike the prior Minnesota statute and the Arkansas statute—are not limited to minority children. The Minnesota Court of Appeals had implied that a racially neutral type of matching statute would be constitutional. An opposite view was expressed recently by the federal district court for Arizona in *Maria Child v. Arizona Department of Economic Security*.[8] It granted a preliminary injunction to parents who alleged that the Arizona Department of Economic Security Policy No. 5-65-09[9] on placement of children with families of the same ethnic or racial backgrounds was in violation of the equal protection clause of the

Fourteenth Amendment. The court held that the policy was unconstitutional because it was "written almost exclusively in racial terms and for that reason is suspect." By its terms, the policy mandates a 90-day period of intensive recruitment for parents of the same racial or ethnic background; only after that delay, and only if no racially similar parents are located, can the agency consider families of other backgrounds. The policy precludes the agency from looking to the merits of nonracially or ethnically matched families "who," the court said, "on balance, may have more to offer the child."

The district court also found the policy unconstitutional as applied. It took evidence on the decision to remove the children and concluded that the only reason for removal was that the children were Hispanic or part Hispanic and the parents were white.

The Indian Child Welfare Act

The Indian Child Welfare Act of 1978 and its virtual prohibition of adoption of Indian children by non-Indians was mentioned earlier, in Chapter 1. This legislation was enacted by Congress under its authority over American Indian affairs, and governs the adoption of Indian children.[10] The most important feature of the Indian Child Welfare Act is that it gives the tribal courts exclusive jurisdiction over child custody proceedings involving children who reside or are domiciled on the reservation, as well as concurrent but presumptive tribal jurisdiction over a child not domiciled on the reservation. The act also contains provisions governing proceedings that take place in state courts. Of these, the most important substantive provision relates to adoptive placements under state law; and the provision mandates,

> In any adoptive placement of an Indian child under state law, a preference shall be given, in the absence of a good cause to the contrary, to a placement with
> (a) a member of the child's extended family;
> (b) other members of the Indian child's tribe; or
> (c) other Indian families.[11]

In *Mississippi Band of Choctaw Indians v. Holyfield*,[12] the U.S. Supreme Court discussed the Indian Child Welfare Act in the context of holding void the adoption of an Indian child by non-Indian parents in a Mississippi state court. The Supreme Court held that the Mississippi court's decree was void for lack of jurisdiction. It found that the act displaced state court jurisdiction in favor of tribal courts even in a case like *Holyfield* where an Indian mother who was domiciled on the reservation gave birth to a child off the reservation, because the domicile of the child follows that of the mother. The Supreme Court recognized that this result protected tribal authority over children born to reservation domiciliaries even where the child's parents sought to avoid tribal authority and to place the child for adoption with a non-Indian couple. The Court found that Congress intended to protect tribal sovereignty over individual Indian choices, quoting the American Indian Policy Review Commission that "removal of Indian children from their cultural setting seriously impacts a long-term tribal survival." This objective of preserving Indian tribes may be found to be the justification for the role race plays in the Indian Child Welfare Act.

Title VI of the 1964 Civil Rights Act

The Civil Rights Act of 1964[13] prohibits discrimination on the ground of race, color, or national origin under any program or activity receiving federal financial assistance. Under that statute and the regulations enacted pursuant to it,[14] the Office of Civil Rights in the U.S. Department of Health and Human Services has issued a policy applicable to adoption and child placements. It provides that the race or ethnicity of a child is a factor that may be considered by an agency receiving federal funds, but it may not be used in an automatic fashion. Each case must be decided on an individual basis so that the best interest of the child is realized. Since most, if not all, state adoption agencies and many private ones receive federal funds—usually under the Adoption Assistance and Child Welfare Act—the civil rights regulations are important.

A citizen can file a complaint with one of the regional offices of the Office of Civil Rights (OCR) throughout the country. The OCR then has an obligation to investigate the agency's policy or practice, to determine if it violates the Civil Rights Act.

An investigator will interview the parties involved, as well as sift through any written documentation of the agency's attitudes or practices with regard to transracial adoption. If problems are found, the agency may volunteer to alter its conduct so as not to offend the OCR policy of nonautomatic use of race in placement decisions. This voluntary compliance may result in a "compliance agreement," which is the name given to the document in which the OCR and the agency come to agree on how future conduct will be structured. If no such agreement is forthcoming, the OCR could, in theory, begin proceedings to withdraw federal funds from the recalcitrant state agency. However, this threat is regarded as more illusory than real, given the insulation surrounding the process—in the form of provision for hearings and judicial review—as well as the fact that the lack of funds would ultimately hurt the most innocent player in this game: the children awaiting adoption.

The OCR does not publish or compile any information for public use on the numbers of complaints or compliance agreements it has processed. Newspaper reports,[15] and information from interviews and from the National Coalition to End Racism in America's Child Care System, suggest that there have been a number of successful complaints about agency practices.

Agency Practice

The role of adoption agencies[16] is so important in the adoption process because, first of all, the formal law—the statutes and case law—is guided by a very general principle: the best interest of the child. It is the experts in what is the best interest of the child in adoption—the adoption agencies—that determine the substance of the law and shape the decisions affecting adoptive parents and children needing homes. When the adoption agency has a policy that says black children are better served in long-term foster care than in white homes, the courts defer to its expertise, usually without much question about the basis for its views. The extent of the courts' deference to agency decisions has been analogized to the deference that courts accord natural parents over decisions concerning their own children.[17]

The second reason why adoption agencies are so powerful in the adoption process comes from the fact that the process of adoption begins long before the matter goes to court. It begins with choosing a home in which to place a child, and with screening prospective adoptive parents. These are all low-visibility decisions difficult to control from within the agency, let alone from outside through judicial review. For example, in one of the states that by statute prohibits the denial of adoption on the basis of race, there is anecdotal evidence that agency social workers have refused to take applications from white couples seeking to adopt black or mixed-race children—clearly a violation of the law.

Although some agency policies are written,[18] they may not be; and even when they are, individual caseworkers may adhere to biases that, as pointed out above, are difficult to identify—let alone control. Despite the acknowledged lack of research at this level of agency practice, there emerges a consensus from the little that has been done: that policies of racial matching constitute the modus operandi for almost all adoption placement decisions.[19] Interestingly, studies done in both 1967 and 1991 confirm this result.

In 1967 Susan Grossman—seeking the answer to why black children's prospects for adoption were much worse than those of white children—surveyed by mail a large number of both public and private adoption agencies. She was interested in whether the situation had changed since a 1954 survey of 250 agencies in which 240 had reported that they considered racial background important, and in which the remaining ten evidenced this fact by their practice—if not by their response to the survey. Grossman's 1967 findings, simply stated, were that "there is little doubt that it [racial matching] is part of the process of most agencies."[20]

In the 1990s, one might be tempted to discount Grossman's work as a result of the time in which her research was conducted. In 1967, many states still had antimiscegenation statutes on their books. It was only later that year that the Supreme Court found them to be unconstitutional.[21] However, research published by Elizabeth Bartholet in 1991 mirrors the conclusions reached by Grossman 24 years earlier. Bartholet's findings are based on a series of interviews with various participants in, or interested observers of, the adoption process. Her conclusion is that racial matching remains the dominant mode of allocating children to homes: "An initial order of business for most adoption agencies is the separation of children and prospective parents into racial classifications and subclassifications."[22] She comments, "This investigation has also made clear that current policies have a severe impact on minority children, often causing serious delays in or permanent denial of adoptive placement."[23]

One of the causes of delay to which Bartholet refers is the "holding policy" to which many agencies informally adhere—though occasionally written guidelines will structure this practice. A holding policy describes a decision by an agency to "hold back" a child in institutional or foster care for a certain period of time, after which, if no in-race placement opportunity has surfaced, transracial adoption may be considered. Though this may initially appear to be a policy that is seeking to walk a middle line between the proponents and objectors to transracial adoption, reality would suggest otherwise. The holding-back period often only begins to run once a child is legally free for adoption—which can often take two to four years if judicial termination of the natural parents' rights is required. Further, even when in theory a child may be placed transracially, often caseworkers will not want to incur the ire of such groups as the National Association of Black Social Workers (NABSW),[24] which tend to protest transracial placements when they become aware of them.

The Case Law

Constitutional Law Background

Since the 1940s, race has been treated by the U.S. Supreme Court as a "suspect classification" under the equal protection clause of the federal Constitution. This means that the use of race in an official decision is subject to strict judicial scrutiny. Racial classifications are valid only when they are justified by a compelling governmental interest and are necessary to the accomplishment of that legitimate state purpose. In 1967 the Court—relying on other cases that applied strict scrutiny analysis—struck down laws prohibiting racial intermarriage, in *Loving v. Virginia.*[25] After that, state laws prohibiting transracial adoption were either repealed by state legislatures or held unconstitutional. In *In re Gomez,*[26] the Texas Court of Appeals reached the conclusion that the law prohibiting transracial adoption violated the federal and Texas constitutions. In *Compos v. McKeithen,*[27] the federal district court for Louisiana held unconstitutional a Louisiana statute that limited adoptions to children of the same race as the adopter.

In 1984 the U.S. Supreme Court looked at a closely related issue: the use of race in a custody decision between divorced parents. In *Palmore v. Sidoti,*[28] a white couple had been divorced and the mother awarded custody of their child. When the mother married a black man, the father sought a change of custody to himself. The trial judge granted the change, saying,

> This court feels that despite the strides that have been made in bettering relations between the races in this country, it is inevitable that Melanie will, if allowed to remain in her present situation and attain school age and thus more vulnerable to peer pressures, suffer from the social stigmatization that is sure to come.[29]

The U.S. Supreme Court reversed. It acknowledged that the child's welfare was the controlling factor, but found that the Florida court had based its decision solely on race: "It is clear that the outcome would have been different had [the mother] married a Caucasian male of similar respectability." It recognized that the Florida court was correct that racial prejudices exist and that "there is a risk that a child living with a stepparent of a different race may be subject to a variety of pressures and stresses not present if the child were living with parents of the same racial or ethnic origin." But it held that "the effects of prejudice, however real, cannot justify a racial classification removing an infant child from the custody of its natural mother found to be an appropriate person to have such custody."

Palmore v. Sidoti involved a custody dispute between the child's natural parents and, therefore, the relevance of this precedent for transracial adoption may be limited. However, the issues are closely enough related that *Palmore* ought not be ignored when considering how the Court might apply the Fourteenth Amendment to an adoption case. Particularly important is the fact that racial considerations were not allowed as part of the best interest of the child analysis.

The Role of Race in Adoption Cases

Prior to the U.S. Supreme Court ruling in *Loving v. Virginia,* which clearly spelled the demise of prohibitions on interracial adoptions, the general rule of the cases in which courts considered the role race should play in adoption decisions was that it may be considered in determining the best interest of the child, but it cannot be controlling.

That rule continues to be the approach of the courts. For example, in *Compos*—the case striking down the Louisiana statute prohibiting transracial adoptions—the court noted that, although recognition of the difficulties of interracial adoption could not justify race as the deciding factor in an adoption, it did justify consideration of race as a relevant factor.

Often the courts do not analyze why race can constitutionally be considered on the issue of the best interest of the child. Based on precedent—that is, the holding of prior cases—they assume the constitutional issue is whether race is the sole determining consideration or only one of the relevant factors. In *Drummond v. Fulton County Department of Family and Children's Services,*[30] the U.S. Court of Appeals for the Fifth Circuit was faced with white foster parents alleging that the denial of their petition to adopt their black foster child was based solely on race and that this violated their right to equal protection. The district court had found that the petition had not been denied solely on the basis of race. The court of appeals did not disturb this finding. However, it recognized that the decision makers had definitely taken the race of the parties into account. Thus, the specific issue was whether this limited use of race was valid. The court concluded that considering race as a factor was constitutionally permissible. It noted that "no case has been cited to the court suggesting that it is impermissible to consider race in adoption placement. The only cases which have addressed this problem indicate that, while the automatic use of race is barred, the use of race as one of the factors in making the ultimate decision is legitimate."

One court has even stated that failure to consider race as one of the relevant factors is error. The case in which the court took that position was *In re Davis*.[31] The court was faced with competing claims for custody from a black couple with whom two siblings of the child had been placed and an elderly white couple who had raised and cared for the black child from three days after his birth until the age of four. The elderly white couple had been denied custody and sought review of the decision. One of the grounds of error they claimed was that the lower court had neglected to consider race as a factor in the decision. The Pennsylvania Supreme Court agreed that a failure to consider race in adoption proceedings was erroneous, but that in the circumstances of this case the error was harmless, as the racial factor would have militated *against* the white couple anyway. In the process of discussing the place of race in adoption decisions, the court said that "critical commentary, as well as near unanimous precedent, overwhelmingly adopt the position that the respective races of the participants is a *factor* to be considered in a child's placement determination but, *as with all factors, can be no more than that—a factor.*"[32]

In a few cases, the courts have applied standard Fourteenth Amendment equal protection analysis and subjected the use of race in the adoption decision to strict scrutiny. Even under that analysis, the courts have found that consideration of race in an adoption is constitutionally acceptable. In *Petition of R.M.G.,*[33] for example, the District of Columbia Court of Appeals—applying strict scrutiny to the District adoption statute—found that the best interest of the child was a compelling state interest and that the race of the child and the adoptive parents was relevant to that compelling state interest. It reasoned that because adoptees often have difficulty with a sense of identity, and because the attitude of the parents toward race—in transracial adoptions—may be highly relevant to the child's sense of identity, those responsible for an adoption decision "will not be able to focus adequately on an adoptive child's sense of identity, and thus on the child's best interest, without considering race."

The court concluded, "In sum, an inherently suspect, indeed presumptively invalid, racial classification in the adoption statute is, in a constitutional sense, necessary to advance a compelling governmental interest: the best interest of the child. It thus survives strict scrutiny— a result that is unusual, as racial classifications go, but not precluded."

In *McLaughin v. Pernsley*,[34] the court granted a preliminary injunction to white foster parents whose black foster child had been removed from their care solely on the basis of race, requiring the City of Philadelphia to return the child. The court found that the goal of providing for the child's racial and cultural needs to effect the best interest of the child was a compelling governmental interest for the purposes of the equal protection clause. However, the court then found that the use of race as the sole criterion for a placement was not necessary to accomplish that compelling state interest. The court held that the decision to remove the black child from the white foster home for placement in a black foster home violated the equal protection rights of the black child and the white foster parents.

Another view of the basic rules governing the use of race in adoptions was expressed by the District of Columbia Court of Appeals in *Petition of D.I.S.*[35] It held that equal protection analysis does not require that strict scrutiny be applied to the use of race in adoption decisions. The District adoption statute, said the court, only requires that information on the race of the petitioner and the child be included in the adoption petition, and does not therefore require that the court give it any consideration. Because the statute does not separate persons solely on the basis of racial declassification or give preference for that reason, it was not subject to strict scrutiny.

Summary of Case Law Discussion

Several points emerge from this discussion of cases dealing with the issue of race in adoption decisions. One is that—contrary to the underlying rule—the courts are very willing to allow race to be considered in adoption placement. Another is that there seems to be no uniform approach to the legal analysis of the consideration of race in adoption; but nevertheless, it is clear that use of race as the sole reason to make or change an adoption placement is condemned under any approach.

Intercountry Adoption

An intercountry adoption—that is, the adoption of a child who is a resident of a foreign country by U.S. parents—requires compliance with three sets of rules:

1. The law of the country of the child's birth. In current adoption practice, this country—which is usually an economically struggling Third World country—is often called either the "sending country" because it sends its children to other (richer) countries for adoption, or the "country of origin" because the children are from that country.
2. The regulations of the Immigration and Naturalization Service (INS), which must be followed so the child will be admitted to the United States.
3. The laws of the state where the adoptive parents live.

Each of these parts of the legal framework for intercountry adoption is described below, followed by a discussion of existing and proposed international adoption treaties.

The Law of the Child's Residence

Most sending countries in international adoptions require that the child be adopted in that country. A few allow proxy adoption, which enables parents to adopt without traveling to the country where the child resides. A few allow the child to leave the sending country to be adopted in the United States. If the country requires that the child be adopted in that country, an international adoption requires that one or both of the prospective parents travel to the sending country and remain there long enough to process the adoption. This can be a long, frustrating, and expensive process.[36] The requirement that an adoption be made in the country of residence is regarded as one of the major problems in intercountry adoptions.

As part of the adoption process, a home study made in the United States by an authorized agency will be required. The country of the child's residence may also require that a local "home study" be conducted in that country.

After the requirements of the sending country are met either through adoption or clearance for placement in the United States, a passport for the child must be obtained from the sending country to enable the child to travel to the United States.

U.S. Immigration Laws

In order for a foreign adoption to be recognized for immigration into the United States, three requirements must be fulfilled.[37] First, the law of the state of the adoptive parents must be satisfied as well as that of the sending country of the child's origin. Second, the parents must be considered suitable to adopt as shown by a home study conducted by an agency approved in the United States. And third, the child must satisfy the U.S. immigration law definition of "orphan." This definition frequently causes problems because it may be much more limited than the group of children legally free for adoption in the foreign country. Persons knowledgeable about intercountry adoption warn there is a real danger that foreign agencies and intermediaries not fully knowledgeable about U.S. immigration law may process the adoptions of children who are legally free for adoption in the foreign country but do not meet the U.S. definition of "orphan."

The Law of the Adoptive Parents' State of Residence

The law of the adoptive parents' state of residence may require the adoptive parents to fulfill certain requirements, regardless of whether the adoption is processed in the foreign country. If the adoption was not finalized in that country, an adoption in the state of the adoptive parents' residence is required. This means complying with the adoption law of that state, which may require a period of residence with the adoptive family prior to finalization of the adoption.

If there was an adoption in the foreign country, it will usually be recognized by the U.S. courts; but adoptive parents are advised to have an adoption in the state of their residence as well, to ensure against legal problems that might arise. Also, it may be useful to have local documents in English attesting to the birth and the adoption and to have those documents readily available with U.S. courts and agencies.[38]

International Treaties

The problems that prospective adoptive parents encounter with international adoptions, and the increasing numbers of those adoptions, have led to considerable interest in negotiating international agreements involving both the countries that provide children for adoption (sending countries, or countries of origin) and those that provide the adopting parents (receiving countries). Since 1984, three treaties dealing with adoptions have been drafted. These are the Inter-American Convention, the UN Human Rights Treaty, and the Hague Convention on Intercountry Adoption.

The Inter-American Convention

In 1984 the Third Inter-American Specialized Conference on Private International Law drew up the Inter-American Convention on Conflict of Laws concerning the Adoption of Minors.[39] Eighteen member states of the Organization of American States (OAS), including the United States, participated in the conference. Of those present, the only states *not* signing the convention on adoption of minors were Nicaragua and Peru.

The Inter-American Convention is limited to those states belonging to the OAS, but it includes both receiving (primarily the United States) and sending states.

The Inter-American Convention places jurisdiction in the sending nations. It is the child's habitual residence that grants adoptions. The laws of the receiving state still apply, but only in establishing the requirements necessary to qualify as an adopter—such as capacity and eligibility.

The Inter-American Convention provides that "adoptions that are in conformity with this Convention shall produce their effects unconditionally in the States Parties."[40] There is an "escape" clause under article 18, which allows for the refusal of applicable law and for a denial of the otherwise legal adoption when deemed "manifestly contrary to the public policy."

The UN Human Rights Treaty

In 1989, the United Nations adopted a convention on human rights that encompassed international adoptions: article 21 of the UN Human Rights Treaty.[41] Article 21 provides safeguards against abuses—such as baby trafficking and sales—and sets standards equivalent to those available for intracountry adoptions. It guarantees that, prior to adoption, the competent authorities have received consent from the biological parents or ensures that abandonment did in fact take place. It emphasizes the desirability of intracountry adoptions over transnational ones and recognizes international adoptions as an alternative only when "the child cannot be placed in a foster or an adoptive family or cannot in any suitable manner be cared for in the child's country of origin." This treaty has not yet been ratified by any member nation.

Hague Convention on Protection of Children and Cooperation in Respect of Intercountry Adoption

In 1988, at the sixteenth session of the Hague Conference, it was decided that at the next session the agenda should include a convention on international adoptions. The Hague Conference on Private International Law is a 36-member body composed mainly of industrialized and developed nations. The seventeenth session met in May 1993, and at that time approved the final text of a Convention on transnational adoptions.[42] The final draft was prepared by the Hague Special Commission on Intercountry Adoption at a meeting in February 1992, and it deserves attention and analysis in the context of past conventions and present-day problems.[43]

The first session of the special commission, in 1990, was attended by 48 nations and a number of nongovernmental international organizations.[44] The strength of this session lay in the participation of Hague member and nonmember states, government and nongovernmental organizations, and sending and receiving countries. The issues discussed at this preparatory meeting included

> fundamental principles and objectives of intercountry adoption and co-operation, the divisions of responsibilities between sending and receiving states, the role of national central authorities, the role of non-governmental adoption agencies and private adoptions and conditions for them, the questions of jurisdiction, applicable law and recognition of foreign adoption decisions, and the handling of such matters as cases where placement or adoption is not successful, trafficking, nationality . . .[45]

Based on these objectives, the Special Commission on Intercountry Adoption prepared several drafts, culminating in a 1992 Preliminary Draft Convention and finally in the 1993 Convention.

The 1993 Convention is the result of three years of investigation, deliberation, and compromise between the members of the commission responsible for its preparation. The skeleton of this initiative comes from the prior work done by Hague commissions and the United Nations. Both article 21 of the UN Human Rights Treaty and the UN Declaration of 1986 are reflected in the document.

The key focus of the 1993 Hague Convention is its attention to the need for cooperation between the sending and receiving countries. It has many strong points. Most important, it includes a large diverse membership. As many as 57 countries have participated in the process. These include not only developed receiving countries, but also about 20 countries that provide the children to be adopted. The 1993 Hague Convention takes into account the differing needs of the sending and receiving states. It seeks to end the baby-selling abuses that have attracted media attention and to curb the more common delays and legal hassles that adoptive parents face. It attempts to establish uniform guidelines for making sure that adoptive parents are suitable, that children who cannot be cared for in their own countries are legally adoptable, and that consent is given freely, irrevocably, and without undue amounts of money changing hands.

By signing this treaty, the nations are expressing their belief that international adoptions under these provisions and safeguards are not contrary to the nations' own public policies. Moreover, this 1993 Intercountry Adoption Convention document puts responsibility not just on the sending state, but also on the receiving country, to guard against any abuses. The document also calls for uniformity among the contracting states, thus eliminating many of the roadblocks to a successful international adoption.

Perhaps the most important innovation of the new convention is that it establishes a "central authority" in each country to deal with the adoption process for children and adoptive applicants. These central authorities are charged with facilitating adoptions. They take applications from adoptive applicants in the receiving states and provide information on adoptable children in the states of origin. The central authorities are directed to cooperate with each other and eliminate obstacles to the application of the treaty.

The final text of the Convention was approved on 29 May 1993 at the seventeenth session of the Hague conference. Now that it is adopted, it must be ratified and implemented by each signatory country. Whether it will be widely implemented is difficult to predict. On the one hand, some Third World countries object to intercountry adoption as "imperialistic, self-serving, and a return to a form of colonialism"[46] and may be unwilling to participate in a process that facilitates such adoptions. On the other hand, officials in some of the receiving countries are concerned that the treaty just adds another level of bureaucracy to the process.

Notes

1. *Drummond v. Fulton County Department of Family and Children's Services,* 568 F.2d 1200 (5th Cir. 1977).

2. For an excellent study of the law and practice of racial matching in adoption, see Elizabeth Bartholet, "Where Do Black Children Belong? The Politics of Race Matching in Adoption," 139 *University of Pennsylvania Law Review* 1163 (1991).

3. There are nine states and the District of Columbia: Col. Rev. Stat., sec. 19-5-208 (1991); D.C. Code, sec. 16-305 (1991); Ill. Rev. Stat., ch. 40, par. 1519.1 (1991); Burns Ind. Code Ann., sec. 31-3-1-1 (Michie 1991); Rev. Stats. Mo., sec. 453.070 (1990); Cons. Laws. N.Y. Ann., art. 7, tit. II, sec. 112 (McKinney 1992); Ohio Rev. Code Ann., sec. 3107.12 (Baldwin 1991); Okla. Rev. Stat., sec. 60.12 (West 1991); S.C. Code Ann., sec. 20-7-1740 (1990); Tex. Stats. Ann. Family Code, sec. 16.032 (West 1991).

4. The National Council for Adoption lists 13 states with racial matching laws. These probably include states with administrative policy statements. See Arizona Department of Economic Security Policy—reproduced in note 9 below—as it appeared in the *Wisconsin State Journal* (June 13, 1992), p. 3A.

5. The wording of the statutes is as follows:

ARK. STAT. ANN., SEC. 9-9-102 (1991)

(b) In the placement or adoption of a child of minority racial or minority ethnic heritage, in reviewing the placement, the court shall consider preference, and in determining appropriate placement, the court shall give preference, in the absence of good cause to the contrary, to:

(1) A relative or relatives of the child, or, if that would be detrimental to the child or a relative is not available;

(2) A family with the same racial or ethnic heritage as the child, or if that is not feasible;

(3) A family of different racial or ethnic heritage from the child which family is knowledgeable and appreciative of the child's racial or ethnic heritage.

CAL. CIV. CODE, SEC. 276 (DEERING, 1991)

Whenever a child is being considered for adoption, the following order of placement preferences regarding racial background or ethnic identification shall be used, subject to the provisions of this title, in determining the adoptive setting in which the child should be placed:

(a) In the home of a relative.

(b) If a relative is not available, or if placement with available relatives is not in the child's best interest, with an adoptive family with the same racial background or ethnic identification as the child. If the child has a mixed racial or ethnic background, placement shall be made with a family of the racial or ethnic group with which the child has the more significant contacts.

(c) If placement cannot be made under the rules set forth in this section within 90 days from the time the child is relinquished for adoption or has been declared free from parental custody or control, the child is free for adoption with a family of a different racial background or ethnic identification where there is evidence of sensitivity to the child's race, ethnicity, and culture.

MINN. STAT., SEC. 259.255 (1991)

The policy of the state of Minnesota is to ensure that the best interests of the child are met by requiring due consideration of the child's minority race or minority ethnic heritage in adoption placements.

The authorized child placing agency shall give preference, in the absence of good cause to the contrary, to placing the child with (a) a relative or relatives of the child, or, if that would be detrimental to the child or a relative is not available, (b) a family with the same racial or ethnic heritage as the child, or, if that is not feasible, (c) a family of different racial or ethnic heritage from the child which is knowledgeable and appreciative of the child's racial or ethnic heritage. [Amended in 1992 to apply to all adoptions and, effective 1 July 1993, to add "not sole" after "due" in the second line. Minnesota now appears to be back in the mainstream on adoption and race.]

6. *Matter of Welfare of D. L.*, 479 N.W.2d 408 (Minn. App. 1991).

7. *Matter of Welfare of D. L.*, 486 N.W.2d 375 (Minn. 1992).

8. Unpublished opinion by Earl H. Carroll, U.S. District Judge, April 9, 1992.

9. The Arizona Department of Economic Security (DES) Policy No. 5-65-09 is so informative that it is reproduced here in full.

A. Policy on placement of children with families of the same ethnic or racial backgrounds.

1. Children being placed for adoption by the department deserve the opportunity for parents of similar ethnic or racial background. It is recognized that identity problems, especially in adolescence, often are encountered by children who are placed outside their racial or ethnic group.

Selection of parents of all children will be based upon the needs of the individual child as outlined in DES 5-65 Exhibit 3. That is, selection will be based upon an assessment of the family's ability to successfully parent the particular child. It will be recognized that successful parenting can and does take many forms within various racial and ethnic groups. Thus, capable adoptive parents can be found in all such groups.

  2. Preference on placement will be as follows:
    a. A member of the child's extended family who meets adoption certification requirements.
    b. Adoptive parents (or single parent) from the same racial or ethnic background of the child.
    For children of racial or ethnic mix, the preference will be:
    i. Adoptive parents (or single parent) from the same racial or ethnic background to which the child most likely will be identified by society as belonging.
    ii. Based on the child's life experiences and preference if age twelve (12) or over.
    NOTE: If there is doubt about which ethnic or racial background of the adoptive family would be most beneficial for the child, a staffing will be held, and will include:
    —The child's case manager and supervisor.
    —The program manager or designee.
    —A central office representative or designee.
    —Workers or community advocates of the ethnic or racial backgrounds of those attributed to the child.
    —Others as appropriate.
    Final decision will be made by the program manager or designee and central office in the event a consensus cannot be reached at the staffing.
    c. One parent (in a two-parent adoptive family) is of the racial or ethnic background of the child.
    For children of racial or ethnic mixture, the preference will be:
    i. One parent (in a two-parent adoptive family) of the racial or ethnic background to which the child most likely will be identified by society as belonging.
    ii. Based on the child's life experiences and preference if age twelve (12) or over.
    NOTE: If there is a doubt about the child's racial or ethnic identity, a staffing will be held. See staffing note DES 5-65-09.A.B.ii.
  3. Immediate recruitment efforts will be made if parent(s) of similar background are not available. See DES 5-65-10.
  4. If, after ninety (90) days of intensive recruitment effort as described in DES 5-65-10, parents of similar background are not identified for a child, families of other backgrounds will be considered. Written verification will be obtained from the State Adoption Registry that a family of similar background who can meet the child's needs has not been recruited.
    NOTE: If questions arise as to appropriateness of a family of the same or similar background, a staffing will be held. See staffing note DES 5-65-09.A.2.b.ii.
  5. In assessing the capability of the adoptive parent(s) of a different ethnic or racial background to provide the child with a sense of identity and respect for his or her own culture, the following factors shall be considered:

a. The extent of the parent(s)' previous and present involvement with others who are of the same background as the child.

b. The amount of opportunity the child would have for involvement with adults and peers of his/her same background.

c. The parent(s)' acceptance of or sensitivity to the child's cultural background.

d. The attitude of the parent(s)' extended families and the impact of that attitude on the family.

e. The ethnic and racial makeup of the parent(s)' neighborhood.

6. Special Circumstances

a. If a child must move from the foster care home before s/he is free for adoption and a foster-adoption placement is necessary, recruitment efforts to the extent legally possible will be provided to locate foster adoptive parents of similar racial or ethnic background. Placement of a child with a family of different ethnic background on a foster-adoption basis must be approved by the program manager or designee prior to placement. Documentation of the reasons why such a move is necessary will be submitted in writing to the program manager, and an approved copy then will be submitted to the State Adoption Registry.

b. If a foster parent(s) of an ethnic background different from that of the foster child wishes to adopt, a staffing will be held. See staffing note DES 5-65-09.A.2.b.ii. Final approval must be given by the program manager or designee. Documentation as to why this is in the child's best interest will be submitted in writing to the program manager. An approved copy then will be submitted to the State Adoption Registry.

Factors to be considered, in addition to those listed in DES 5-65-09.A.5, are:

i. Availability of minority families who could meet the child's needs, including documented recruitment efforts.

ii. The child's wishes, if the child is over age twelve (12).

iii. Length of placement with the family. Any placement of less than three (3) years should be examined closely to weigh the benefits of remaining with the foster family versus exposure to the parent(s) of the child's own ethnic or racial background.

iv. The quality of care and the quality of the relationship between the foster parent(s) and the child.

v. Attempts by the foster parent(s) to help the child develop identity, taking into account possible adolescent and adult identity problems.

10. The Indian Child Welfare Act of 1978 is codified at 25 U.S.C., secs. 1901ff.

11. Ibid., sec. 1915(a).

12. *Mississippi Band of Choctaw Indians v. Holyfield,* 109 S.Ct. 1597 (1989).

13. The Civil Rights Act of 1964 is codified at 42 U.S.C., sec. 2000d.

14. These regulations are found in 45 C.F.R. 80.

15. See, for example, "White Foster Parents Battle Indiana's Policy against Transracial Adoption," describing complaints filed with the OCR. *Chicago*

Tribune, March 2, 1992, p. 8C. See also, Bartholet, "Where Do Black Children Belong?" p. 1239, n. 212.

16. For an excellent description and discussion of agency practice in adoption, see Jacqueline Macaulay and Stewart Macaulay, "Adoption for Black Children: A Case Study of Expert Discretion," 1 *Research in Law and Sociology* 265 (1978).

17. Patricia W. Ballard, "Racial Matching and the Adoption Dilemma: Alternatives for the Hard to Place," 17 *Journal of Family Law* 333, 353 (1978/79).

18. An example of a written agency policy is the Arizona one that is reproduced in note 9 above.

19. See Bartholet, "Where Do Black Children Belong?"

20. Susan J. Grossman, "A Child of a Different Color: Race as a Factor in Adoption and Custody Proceedings," 17 *Buffalo Law Review* 303 (1967).

21. *Loving v. Virginia,* 338 U.S. 1 (1966).

22. Bartholet, "Where Do Black Children Belong?" p. 1186.

23. Ibid., p. 1185.

24. NABSW constitutes the most well known organized resistance to the practice of transracial adoption. They are famous for a statement they issued in 1972, in which they declared the practice of transracial adoption to be a "form of genocide."

25. *Loving v. Virginia,* 388 U.S. 1 (1967).

26. *In re Gomez,* 424 S.W.2d 656 (Texas 1967).

27. *Compos v. McKeithen,* 341 F.Supp. 264 (E.D. La., 1972).

28. *Palmore v. Sidoti,* 466 U.S. 429 (1984).

29. Ibid., p. 433.

30. *Drummond v. Fulton County Department of Family and Children's Services,* 568 F.2d 1200 (5th Cir. 1977).

31. *In re Davis,* 465 A.2d 614 (Pa. 1983).

32. Ibid., at 622; emphasis in the original.

33. *Petition of R. M. G.,* 454 A.2d 776 (D.C. App. 1982).

34. *McLaughin v. Pernsley,* 693 F. Supp. 318 (E.D. Pa. 1988).

35. *Petition of D. I. S.,* 494 A.2d 1316 (D.C. App. 1985).

36. See, for example, "Ordeal in Peru: Cuddling a Baby, Clinging to Hope," *New York Times,* June 9, 1992, p. A7.

37. Elizabeth Bartholet, "International Adoption Overview," in *Adoption Laws and Practices,* ed. J. Hollinger (New York: Matthew Bender, 1991), pp. 30–31.

38. Ibid., pp. 10-32.

39. Inter-American Convention on Conflict of Laws concerning the Adoption of Minors, Third Inter-American Specialized Conference on Private International Law (CIDIP-III), General Assembly of the Organization of American States, La Paz, Bolivia, May 15–24, 1984, reprinted in J. H. A. Van Loon, *Report on Intercountry Adoption,* Hague Conference on Private International Law, Netherlands, April 1990; pp. 170–74.

40. Inter-American Convention, article 5.51.

41. UN Human Rights Treaty, 1989, printed in Van Loon, *Report,* pp. 180–84; also Cynthia Cohen and Howard Davidson, *Children's Rights in America* (Chicago: American Bar Association, 1991), p. xix.

42. See J. H. A. Van Loon, *Report,* n. 27 at 2–10.

43. Preliminary Draft Convention on International Cooperation and Protection of Children in Respect of Intercountry Adoption, Special Commission on Intercountry Adoption, Hague Conference on Private International Law, Netherlands, February 1992.

44. American Embassy, the Hague, to U.S. Secretary of State, Document of First Session of Hague Conference Special Commission on Intercountry Adoption, Netherlands, June 19, 1990.

45. Ibid.

46. UN Department of International Economics and Social Affairs, Report of an Expert Group Meeting on Adoption and Foster Placement of Children, 1980, cited in H. Bogard, "Who Are the Orphans? Defining Orphan Status and the Need for an International Convention on Intercountry Adoption," 5 *Emory International Law Review* 571 (1991).

Political considerations, rich versus poor countries and developed versus undeveloped ones, concerns by countries about "exporting" their children, and concerns about differing racial and cultural backgrounds all raise questions about how successful the treaty—no matter how well drafted it is—will be in obtaining national approvals. A widely adopted treaty on international adoptions does not seem imminent.

3

The Case against
Transracial Adoption

In contrast to the evidence on which the case *for* transracial adoptions
rests, the case *against* transracial adoptions is built primarily on
ideology and rhetoric. As the materials in this chapter demonstrate,
there is no empirical or scientific evidence to demonstrate that transracial adoptions work against the best interests of children. What the
anti–transracial adoption side has done is to issue a lot of warnings,
predictions, fears, and threats: "The United States is a racist society";
"White families, even with the best of intentions, cannot teach black
children how to cope and survive in such a society"; "Black children
reared in white homes will grow up to be 'oreos,' black on the outside,
white on the inside"; "Transracial adoption is a massive conspiracy
on the part of the white community to steal black children." This
chapter reports the anti–transracial adoption case as it has been
enunciated and recorded since 1971.

Organized opposition to transracial adoption—begun in the early
part of the 1970s—was formidable enough by 1975 to bring about a
reversal in policy on the part of major adoption agencies in most states
throughout the country. The opposition was led and organized primarily by the National Association of Black Social Workers (NABSW) and
by leaders of black political organizations, who said they saw in the
practice an insidious scheme for depriving the black community of its
most valuable future resource: its children.

Opposition also came from some of the leaders of Native American
groups, who labeled transracial adoption "genocide" and who also
accused white society of perpetuating its most malevolent scheme,
that of seeking to deny the Native Americans their future by taking
away their children.

Both the black and Native American groups who were opposed to transracial adoption agreed that it would be impossible for white parents to rear black or Indian children in an environment that would permit them to retain or develop a black or Indian identity. Even if some white parents might want their adopted children to grow up Indian or black, they would lack the skills, insights, and experience necessary to accomplish such a task.

Black American Opposition

At its national conference in 1971, the president of the NABSW, William T. Merritt, announced, "Black children should be placed only with black families, whether in foster care or for adoption."[1] The following excerpt—beginning with this now well-known announcement—establishes the flavor of the speech.

> Black children should be placed only with Black families, whether in foster care or adoption. Black children belong physically, psychologically and culturally in Black families in order that they receive the total sense of themselves and develop a sound projection of their future. . . . Black children in white homes are cut off from the healthy development of themselves as Black people. The socialization process for every child begins at birth. Included in the socialization process is the child's cultural heritage which is an important segment of the total process. This must begin at the earliest moment; otherwise our children will not have the background and knowledge which is necessary to survive in a racist society. This is impossible if the child is placed with white parents in a white environment. . . .
>
> We [the members of the NABSW] have committed ourselves to go back to our communities and work to end this particular form of genocide [transracial adoption].[2]

In his testimony before a Senate committee on June 25, 1985, Merritt reiterated the NABSW position.

> We are opposed to transracial adoption as a solution to permanent placement for Black children. We have an ethnic, moral and professional obligation to oppose transracial adoption. We are therefore *legally* justified in our efforts to protect the right of Black children, Black families, and the Black community. We view the placement of Black children in White homes as a hostile act against our community. It is a blatant form of race and cultural genocide.[3]

In addition, Merritt made the following claims:

• Black children who grow up in white families suffer severe identity problems. On the one hand, the white community has not fully accepted them; and on the other hand, they have no significant contact with black people.

• Black children adopted transracially often do not develop the coping mechanisms necessary to function in a society that is inherently racist against African Americans.

• Transracial adoptions, in the long term, often end in disruption; and the black children are returned to foster care.

Merritt provided no evidence for the above claims.

At the annual meeting of the Black Adoption Committee for Kids on November 8, 1991, another former president of the National Association of Black Social Workers, Morris Jeff, Jr., stated,

> Placing African-American children in white European-American homes is an overt hostility, the ultimate insult to black heritage. It is the creation of a race of children with African faces and European minds. It is a simple answer to a complex situation. It causes more problems than it solves.[4]

In 1974, the Black Caucus of the North American Conference on Adoptable Children recommended "support [for] the consciousness development movement of all groups" and "that every possible attempt should be made to place black and other minority children in a cultural and racial setting similar to their original group."[5] In May 1975, the dean of the Howard University School of Social Work and president of the NABSW stated that "black children who grow up in white homes end up with white psyches."[6]

In one of the more moderate attacks on transracial adoption, Leon Chestang in 1972 posed a series of critical questions for white parents who had adopted or who were considering adopting a black child.

> The central focus of concern in biracial adoption should be the prospective adoptive parents. Are they aware of what they are getting into? Do they view their act as purely humanitarian, divorced from its social consequences? Such a response leaves the adoptive parents open to an overwhelming shock when friends and family reject and condemn them. Are they interested in building world brotherhood without recognizing the personal consequences for the child placed in such circumstances? Such people are likely to be well meaning but unable to relate to the

child's individual needs. Are the applicants attempting to solve a personal or social problem through biracial adoption? Such individuals are likely to place an undue burden on the child in resolving their problems.[7]

And what of the implications for the adoptive family itself of living with a child of another race? Chestang asked. Are negative societal traits attributed to blacks likely to be passed on to the adoptive family, thereby subjecting the family to insults, racial slurs, and ostracism?

The white family that adopts a black child is no longer a "white family." In the eyes of the community, its members become traitors, nigger-lovers, do-gooders, rebels, oddballs, and, most significantly, ruiners of the community. Unusual psychological armaments are required to shield oneself from the behavioral and emotional onslaught of these epithets.[8]

But Chestang concluded his piece on a more optimistic note than most critics of transracial adoption. "Who knows what problems will confront the black child reared by a white family and what the outcome will be?" he asked. "But these children, if they survive, have the potential for becoming catalysts for society in general."[9]

Most black writers opposed to transracial adoption challenged two main hypotheses: (1) that there are insufficient black adoptive parents willing to adopt black children; and (2) that the benefits a black child will receive in a white family surpass those received in an institution. They observed that many potential nonwhite adoptive parents are disqualified because of adoption agencies' widespread use of white middle-class criteria for selection. They also noted that blacks historically have adopted informally, preferring not to rely on agencies and courts for sanction. Therefore, the figures cited by agencies cannot reflect the actual number of black adoptions. And they claimed that no longitudinal outcome data were available to show that transracial adoption of black children outweighed the known disadvantages of an institution or foster care; they predicted family and personal problems as the children grew into preadolescence and adolescence. A leading black organization pointed to transracially adopted black children who were being returned to foster care because the adoption was not "working out," or were being placed in residential treatment by their white adoptive parents who could not manage them.

Amuzie Chimuzie attributed "all consciously motivating human actions"—for example, transracial adoption—to "selfish needs."[10] He argued that young children are rarely consulted when a major decision is to be made in their lives and that this sense of powerlessness is exacerbated for a young black child in a white adoptive family. Chimuzie suggested,

It seems appropriate that blacks collectively as parents should speak for the black child in matters touching transracial adoption. . . . It is up to the agent of the child—in this instance blacks as a group—to accept or reject it [transracial adoption]. . . . [I]t has not been determined whether a majority of the blacks are for or against transracial adoption of black children.[11]

One of the most prevalent arguments against transracial adoption is that white families—no matter how liberal or well intended—cannot teach a black child how to survive in an essentially racist society. Nonwhites opposed to transracial adoption insist that, because white adoptive parents are not black and cannot experience minority black status, they will rear a psychologically defenseless individual, incapable of understanding and dealing with the racism that exists in our society. Amuzie Chimuzie articulated this position when he emphasized the fear of black social workers and other experts in the child-rearing field that black children reared in white homes will not develop the characteristics needed to survive and flourish in a predominantly white society. After first observing that children tend to acquire most of the psychological and social characteristics of the families and communities in which they are reared, Chimuzie added, "It is therefore possible that black children reared in white families and communities will develop antiblack psychological and social characteristics."[12]

Some black professionals argue that there is a major bottleneck in the placement of black children in black adoptive homes, and this is because child welfare agencies are staffed mainly by white social workers who exercise control over adoptions. The fact that these white agencies are in the position of recruiting and approving black families for adoption causes some blacks to argue that there is institutional racism on the part of the whites. In contrast, there have been several instances where concerted efforts by black child welfare agencies to locate and approve adoptive black families resulted in the adoption of comparatively large numbers of parentless black children.

The above position was strongly argued by Evelyn Moore, executive director of the National Black Child Development Institute.[13] In an extensive interview on the child welfare system published by the National Association of Social Workers (NASW) in April 1984—a

significant part of which dealt either directly or indirectly with TRA—
Moore said that 83 percent of all child welfare workers in the United
States are white, while 30–40 percent of their cases deal with black
families. This skewed ratio, she contends, is one of the reasons that
there are so few in-racial black adoptions. "The adoption system in
this country was established to provide white children to white families. As a result, most people who work in the system know very little
about black culture or the black community."[14]

Moore also argued that "white middle-class standards" are largely
responsible for the rejection of lower-class and working-class black
families as potential adopters; they are instead encouraged to become
foster parents: "While black children under the age of 19 represent
only 14 percent of the children in America, they represent 33 percent
of all children not living with their birth parents" (e.g., in foster care
or institutionalized).[15]

Two studies conducted by the National Urban League in 1984 are
cited by black professionals and organizations as further evidence of
the likelihood that institutional racism is one of the primary reasons
that more black children are not given to prospective black adoptive
families.[16] These studies reported that, of 800 black families applying
for adoptive parent status, only two families were approved—0.25
percent—as compared to a national average of 10 percent. Another
study concluded that 40–50 percent of the black families sampled
would consider adoption. An acceptance rate of 0.25 percent becomes
somewhat more dramatic when compared to black in-racial adoption
rates of 18 per 10,000 families. (The figures for whites and Hispanics
are four and three per 10,000 families, respectively.)

In a 1987 *Ebony* article entitled "Should Whites Adopt Black Children?" the president of the NABSW was quoted as follows: "Our
position is that the African-American family should be maintained and
its integrity preserved. We see the lateral transfer of black children to
white families as contradictory to our preservation efforts."[17]

The article also reported that many of those who oppose transracial
adoption see it as "tantamount to racial and cultural genocide" and
claim that "there's no way a black child can develop as a total black
person if s/he lives in a white family."[18] To counterbalance these
statements, the article quoted several paragraphs from *Transracial
Adoptees and Their Families* by Rita Simon and Howard Altstein,[19] in
which we stated that our data did not suggest these children were lost
to the black community, and that the fear of some blacks about
transracially adopted black children developing into racially confused

adolescents and adults had not been realized. The *Ebony* article ended on a hopeful note, stating that "the challenge before us is one of extending successful black adoption programs and ultimately, creating a new society in which the racial identity of potential adoptive parents (black and white) is irrelevant."[20]

In 1986, the founder of Homes for Black Children—a successful black adoption agency in Detroit—issued the following statement:

> I believe it was the convergence of these two diverse movements, the transracial adoption movement and the one on the part of Black people to affirm our ability to care for ourselves and our children . . . that resulted in the clash. . . .
>
> For those of us who are Black, the pain has been the fear of losing control of our own destiny through the loss of our children. . . .
>
> . . . [T]here is real fear, in the hearts of some of us who are Black, as to whether a child who is Black can be protected in this society, without the protection of families who are most like him. . . . [A] Black child is especially endangered when agencies or programs that are successful in finding Black families are not available to meet his need.[21]

The winter 1989 newsletter of Homes for Black Children carried a response to the above statement, written by a member of an Ohio organization called Adopting Older Kids.

> Nowhere in this statement is there acknowledgment of the adoptive parents whose love transcends racial boundaries. . . . Nor are there suggestions about the future of those minority children, already waiting for families, who will be denied loving homes because agencies refuse to consider transracial placements.[22]

How can one explain the discrepancy between the apparently widespread desire to adopt among blacks and the dearth of approved black homes for adoption? First of all, blacks have not adopted in the expected numbers because child welfare agencies have not actively recruited in black communities, using community resources, the black media, and churches. Second, there is a historic suspicion of public agencies among many blacks, the consequence of which is that many restrict their involvement with them. Third, many blacks feel that, no matter how close they come to fulfilling the criteria established for adoption, the fact that many reside in less affluent areas makes the likelihood of their being approved slight.

In 1987, the Council for a Black Economic Agenda—a group dedicated to advancing social welfare policies relevant to the black community—met with President Ronald Reagan to discuss what they and other black groups see as unfair practices on the part of adoption agencies. Urging that eligibility criteria for adoption such as marital status, income, and adoption fees be reexamined with an eye toward more black-oriented standards, they said, "The kind of standards that are being applied by these traditional agencies discriminate against Black parents."[23]

In 1988, the North American Council on Adoptable Children (NACAC) issued the following ten-point "Minority Placement Position Statement."

MINORITY PLACEMENT POSITION STATEMENT

Although it has been demonstrated that there are numerous family resources within Black, Hispanic, and Native American communities, children are denied permanent homes because potentially available resources of the same race are not fully utilized.

NACAC believes that education and commitment must be a priority on a local and federal level so that Black, Hispanic and Native American children are not denied the right to be placed with families of the same race and culture.

In order to tap these family resources, timely and appropriate recruitment and retention programs are needed.

We as the national network of parent groups must advocate at the federal, state, and local levels for:

1. Adequate policy development and funding for all components of adoption services.
2. Full implementation of legislation such as Adoption Assistance and Child Welfare Act of 1980 and Indian Child Welfare Act of 1978.
3. Independent monitoring of allocation of funding and implementation of programs.
4. Objective evaluation of effectiveness of services.
5. Holding agency and governmental entities accountable for outcomes of orientation, assessment, and placement services.
6. Partnership with the minority communities in recruitment, assessment and placement of children in appropriate, culturally relevant homes.
7. Adequate policy and funding supports for relative and extended placements.
8. Placement of children in need of foster care with foster families of the same race/culture as many of these become the child's permanent home through adoption.
9. Adequate training for adoption workers to sensitize and enhance

their knowledge of identity, cultural and ethnic issues in working with Black, Hispanic, and Native American clients.

10. Recruitment of Black, Hispanic, and Native American social workers in the field.[24]

In the second paragraph and in Articles 6 and 8, NACAC appears to rule out the option of cross-racial placement for nonwhite children. These statements take it for granted that racially similar homes would be available.

Native American Opposition

The case of Native Americans is a special one. Native Americans have been subjected to a singularly tragic fate, and their children have been particularly vulnerable. Chapter 1 reported the large number of Native American children believed to have been adopted by white families since 1968.

By the early 1970s, committees of Native Americans joined in the denunciation of transracial adoption. In 1972, a group of Native Americans issued the following statement:

The identity crisis of adolescence is likely to be especially traumatic for the Indian child growing up in a White home. When they are old enough to realize that they're different, there is likely to be real trouble, especially if White parents haven't made serious efforts to expose them to their own cultural heritage. . . . And trouble will come from the White family, too, they say. The White man's hatred of the native American may be forgotten when he's a cute helpless baby or child, but it will show up when the child becomes an adolescent and able to think and act as an individual.[25]

In 1978 Congress passed the Indian Child Welfare Act (P. L. 95-608)—cited in Chapter 2—which was designed to prevent the decimation of Indian tribes and the breakdown of Indian families by transracial placement of Native American children.

In essence, the leaders of Black American and Native American organizations argued that nonwhite children who are adopted by white parents are lost to the communities into which they were born. The experience of growing up in a white world makes it impossible for black and Indian children ever to take their rightful place in the communities of their birth.

Concluding Remarks

Very few, if any, responsible organizations or individuals argue that transracial adoption is preferable to in–racial adoption. Were there sufficient black families for all black children, Hispanic families for Hispanic children, Asian families for Asian children, and so forth, there probably would be no need for transracial adoption. Efforts should be increased to locate minority families—and especially black families—for these children. Those efforts will no doubt be welcomed and supported by all reasonable people. "Traditional" agency policies and practices based on bygone white middle-class assumptions should be altered to meet the current realities of nonwhite communities, thereby increasing the likelihood that larger numbers of potential minority adopters would be located. Such alterations in policies should be promoted by child welfare advocates.

Most—if not all—who see transracial adoption as a viable arrangement see it only when a child's only other options are nonpermanent types of placements such as foster care or group homes. In fact, rarely (if ever) are arguments heard in favor of transracial adoption that do not define it as second-best to permanent in-racial placement and do not also include strong support for community agencies to recruit minority adoptive parents vigorously. Witness the following declarations.

The Child Welfare League of America (CWLA) in its most recently published *Standards for Adoption Service* reaffirmed once again, as it has consistently done in the past, that transracial adoption should be considered only after all efforts at in-racial placement have been exhausted. Under the title "Factors in Selection of Family: Ethnicity and Race," the standards read as follows:

> Children in need of adoption have a right to be placed into a family that reflects their ethnicity or race. Children should not have their adoption denied or significantly delayed, however, when adoptive parents of other ethnic or racial groups are available.
> . . . In any adoption plan, however, the best interests of the child should be paramount. If aggressive, ongoing recruitment efforts are unsuccessful in finding families of the same ethnicity or culture, other families should be considered.[26]

Another example in which transracial adoption is the second choice to in-racial placements appears in a statement made by Father George Clements, a noted black clergyman and founder of "One Church, One Child," a national plan whereby one family from each black church would adopt a black child. After stating that in-racial adoptions were preferable to transracial adoption, Father Clements added, "But you cannot always have the ideal, and in lieu of the ideal, certainly I would opt for an Anglo couple, or whatever nationality, taking a child in."[27]

By the beginning of the 1990s, it appears that the major child welfare and adoption organizations remain strongly committed to the idea of recruiting minority adoptive parents for similar children. In all likelihood, these agencies would abandon support for transracial adoption were there a sufficient number of racially similar parents to accommodate waiting nonwhite children.

In some cases, however, organizations such as the National Association of Black Social Workers continue to cling to the policy that race should be the primary determinant of a child's placement, even if the child has already been placed with and integrated into a family of another race. Support for the concept of in-racial placement in these cases would seem to work against the child's best interest.

So determined is the NABSW to end the practice of placing black children in white homes that they proposed that the 1993 Congress enact an "African American Child Welfare Act" modeled along the lines of the Indian Child Welfare Act. The NABSW would like to see "African American" substituted for "Indian" in their proposed bill, which would thereby forbid by statute the adoption of black children by nonblack families. Should their efforts prove successful, it will relegate even greater numbers of black children to years of foster care or institutionalized living. Black children will thus be deprived of stable and caring family life on the basis of their race.

Notes

1. William T. Merritt, speech to the National Association of Black Social Workers National Conference, Washington, D.C., 1971.

2. Ibid.

3. Excerpt from testimony by William T. Merritt, president of the National Association of Black Social Workers, Senate Hearings, Committee on Labor and Human Resources, June 25, 1985.

4. Morris Jeff, Jr., "Interracial Adoptions Wrong, Says Official," *St. Louis Post Dispatch*, November 9, 1991.

5. "Barriers to Same Race Placement," report of the North American Council on Adoptable Children, St. Paul, Minn., 1991.

6. Sandy Barnesky, "The Question: Is It Bad for Black Children to Be Adopted by Whites?" *Baltimore Sun*, May 28, 1975, p. B1.

7. Leon Chestang, "The Dilemma of Bi-racial Adoption," *Social Work* (May 1972), pp. 100–105.

8. Ibid., p. 103.

9. Ibid., p. 105.

10. Amuzie Chimuzie, "Transracial Adoption of Black Children," *Social Work* (July 1975), pp. 296–301.

11. Ibid., p. 298.

12. Ibid., p. 300.

13. Evelyn Moore, "Black Children Facing Adoption Barriers," *NASW News* (April 1984), p. 9.

14. Ibid., p. 9.

15. Ibid., p. 10.

16. Ibid., p. 11.

17. Morris Jeff, "Should Whites Adopt Black Children?" *Ebony* (September 1987), p. 78.

18. Ibid., p. 78.

19. Rita Simon and Howard Altstein, *Transracial Adoptees and Their Families* (New York: John Wiley and Sons, 1977).

20. Ibid., p. 80.

21. Statement in *Homes for Black Children*, newsletter of Homes for Black Children, Detroit, Mich., 1986.

22. *Homes for Black Children*, Winter, 1989.

23. Council for a Black Economic Agenda, press release on meeting with President Ronald Reagan, Washington, D.C., 1987.

24. Statement of the North American Council on Adoptable Children, Washington, D.C., 1988.

25. *Ann Arbor (Mich.) News*, July 17, 1972, p. 10.

26. *Standards for Adoption Service*, Child Welfare League of America, New York, 1988.

27. Statement of Father George Clements, *The National Adoption Report*, vol. 10, no. 3. Washington, D.C. May–June 1989.

4

The Case for
Transracial Adoption:
Empirical Studies of Transracial
and Intercountry Adoptions

The case for transracial adoption rests primarily on the results of
empirical research. Much of that research is reviewed in this chapter
and in Chapter 5. The data show that transracial adoptions clearly
satisfy the "best interest of the child" standard. They show that
transracial adoptees grow up emotionally and socially adjusted, and
aware of and comfortable with their racial identity. They perceive
themselves as integral parts of their adopted families, and they expect
to retain strong ties to their parents and siblings in the future.

Thus, there is a basic difference in the type and quality of the
arguments that are made for and against transracial adoption. The
latter are based almost completely on rhetoric and ideology. The
National Association of Black Social Workers have never presented
scientific data to support their position. They have described vignettes,
issued warnings, and made dire predictions. For example, after the
findings from the first phase of the Simon–Altstein study were published in 1977—which showed that the transracial adoptees surveyed
were aware of their racial identities and adjusted into their adoptive
families—the NABSW reacted with a warning: wait until these children
become adolescents; then the trouble will start. Other studies and our
subsequent work did not support those predictions. The findings in our
study, as we show in this review of the literature, were not unique or
even unusual. All of the studies—even those carried out by researchers
who were initially skeptical—arrived at the same general conclusions.

Studies of Transracial Adoption within the United States

The work of Lucille Grow and Deborah Shapiro of the Child Welfare League represent one of the earliest studies of transracial adoption. Published in 1974, the major purpose of *Black Children, White Parents* was to assess how successful the adoption by white parents of black children had been.[1] Their respondents consisted of 125 families. The authors measured successful adoptions as follows:

> The question is whether children are better off adopted by parents of a different race than they would be if they lived with neither natural nor adoptive parents. To answer that would necessitate following up black children who had been adopted by white parents and children comparable with the adoptees in all respects except that they had not been adopted. Identifying a comparable sample of nonadopted children did not seem possible.
>
> We, therefore, confined the research to a descriptive study of adoptions of black or part-black children by white parents. We decided to focus on children who were at least six years of age so that they would have had some experience in the community, and on children who had been in their adoptive homes at least three years, long enough for initial adjustments to be worked out.[2]

Later, in discussing the specific measures of success they relied on, Grow and Shapiro discussed the techniques employed by other social work researchers who had been confronted with similar problems. They commented,

> This study of black children adopted by white parents shares the common problem of adoption studies—indeed, of most studies of social programs—that of identifying a valid, operational definition of "success." In an ideal society all adopted children, like their biological peers, would have a happy childhood and develop into well-adjusted, well-functioning adults. In a much-less-than-ideal society, it is evident that many, like their biological peers, will not. Since they do not all become "successful" adults, a series of difficult, usually unanswerable, questions is raised. Is the failure necessarily related to the fact of adoption? Is the rate of failure any different from that observed in the rearing of children by their biological parents? Are the problems of rearing adopted children essentially those inherent in the child-rearing process and subject to the same risks or are they greater? In the specific type of adoption under scrutiny here, is a black child more "successful" in a white adoptive home than he would have been in a black foster home or a series of them?[3]

In the end, Grow and Shapiro decided on the following measures: (1) the child's responses to the California Test of Personality and the Missouri Children's Behavior Check List Test; (2) three scores based on physical and mental symptoms reported by the parents as present or absent in their child; (3) significant adults' evaluation of the child, that is, mother, father, teachers, and parents' assessment of the child's relations with her or his siblings; and (4) the parents' assessment of the child's attitude toward race.

On the basis of the children's scores on the California Test of Personality (which purports to measure social and personal adjustment), Grow and Shapiro concluded that the children in their study made about as successful an adjustment in their adoptive homes as other nonwhite children had in prior studies. They claimed that 77 percent of their children had adjusted successfully, and that this percentage was similar to that reported in other studies.

Grow and Shapiro also compared the scores of transracially adopted children with those of adopted white children on the California Test of Personality. A score below the twentieth percentile was defined as reflecting poor adjustment, and a score above the fiftieth percentile was defined as indicating good adjustment. They found that the scores of their transracially adopted children and those of white adopted children matched very closely.

When the parents were questioned about their expectations concerning their adoptive children's adjustment after adolescence and about the children's ties to the home when they became adults, the responses were generally optimistic. One-third of the parents did not anticipate that their adoptive children would experience future difficulties; 18 percent did not believe that any trouble lay ahead.

When the parents were asked why they chose to adopt a nonwhite child, 54 percent of the parents gave reasons and motivations that were essentially social. Forty-two percent said they wanted to provide a home for a hard-to-place child, and 10 percent characterized transracial adoption as a "Christian act." Forty-nine percent of the mothers and 60 percent of the fathers felt that one benefit of transracial adoption was that they were able to "give a home to a child whom nobody seemed to want."[4] Seventy-one percent of the mothers and 66 percent of the fathers felt that transracial adoption enabled them "to express the deep love for children . . . [they] . . . have always had." Reinforcing the latter statement, and weighed against the idea of transracial adoption as a gesture to right society's wrongs, was the evidence supplied by the parents that "helping to compensate for the inequities in our society" was not perceived to be very much of a benefit of transracial adoption.

Eighty-three percent of the mothers and 82 percent of the fathers said they were not concerned about how their neighbors would react to their adopting a nonwhite child. But about half of the parents were concerned about how their extended families would react to a transracial adoption.

In seeking to find out more about how these parents felt about the concept of transracial adoption, Grow and Shapiro described four types of transracial adoptions and asked which type the parent would encourage or discourage. An "unsure" category was also allowed. As shown in Table 4.1, 91 percent of the mothers and 87 and 83 percent of the fathers would encourage transracial adoption by white and black parents of either part-black or part-white children, respectively. More uncertainty existed with regard to the other two types of adoption.

Fifty-five percent of the parents who felt some anxiety or had some reservation about the adoption also believed that their adopted child felt some discomfort about being adopted, in contrast to 20 percent of the parents who felt no anxiety about their decision to adopt.

In 1977, Joyce Ladner—using the membership lists of the Open Door Society and the Council on Adoptable Children as her sample frames—conducted in-depth interviews with 136 parents in Georgia, Missouri, Washington, D.C., Maryland, Virginia, Connecticut, and Minnesota.[5] Before reporting her findings, she introduced a personal note.

This research brought with it many self-discoveries. My initial feelings were mixed. I felt some trepidation about studying white people, a new undertaking for me. Intellectual curiosity notwithstanding, I had the gnawing sensation that I shouldn't delve too deeply because the findings might be too controversial. I wondered too if the couples I intended to interview would tell me the truth. Would some lie in order to cover up their mistakes and disappointments with the adoption? How much would they leave unsaid? Would some refuse to be interviewed because of their preconceived notions about my motives? Would they stereotype me as a hostile black sociologist who wanted to "prove" that these adoptions would produce mentally unhealthy children?

Prior to starting the interviews I admit to having been skeptical about whether the adoptions could work out well. Because I was reared in the Deep South, with all of its rigid racial segregation, transracial adoption represented, for me, an inexplicable departure from custom and tradition. I would have thought it just as unorthodox for a black couple to adopt a

Table 4.1 Parental Convictions about Transracial Adoptions, 1974 CWLA Study

Racial Characteristics	Mothers			Fathers		
	Encourage	Unsure	Discourage	Encourage	Unsure	Discourage
			(in percent)			
Whites adopting all-black children	65	25	10	67	23	10
Blacks adopting all-white children	59	27	14	61	27	12
Whites adopting part-black children	91	8	1	87	12	1
Blacks adopting part-white children	91	8	1	83	14	3

Source: Lucille J. Grow and Deborah Shapiro, *Black Children, White Parents: A Study of Transracial Adoption* (New York: Child Welfare League of America, 1974), p. 87, table 3-7.

white child. Racial polarization in America sensitizes everyone to the potential hazards in this kind of "mixing" of the races. On the other hand, I was also unwilling to accept the facile cliches the critics use to describe the motives of the adoptive parents. I wanted to find out for myself what kinds of people were adopting and why they did it. What were their day-to-day experiences? How did the adoption affect their biological children? How were the children coping? It was also important to find out the reactions of their families, friends, and neighbors; their philosophies on race relations and black identity; their experiences with the adoption agencies; and their hopes and expectations for their children's future.[6]

By the end of her study, Ladner was convinced that "there are whites who are capable of rearing emotionally healthy black children."[7] Such parents, Ladner continued, "must be idealistic about the future but also realistic about the society in which they now live."

To deny that racial, ethnic, and social class polarization exists, and to deny that their child is going to be considered a "black child," regardless of how light his or her complexion, how sharp their features, or how straight their hair, means that these parents are unable to deal with reality, as negative as they may perceive that reality to be. On the other hand, it is equally important for parents to recognize that no matter how immersed they become in the black experience, they can never become black. Keeping this in mind, they should avoid the pitfalls of trying to practice an all-black lifestyle, for it too is unrealistic in the long run, since their family includes blacks and whites and should, therefore, be part of the larger black and white society.[8]

Charles Zastrow's doctoral dissertation, published in 1977, compared the reactions of 41 white couples who had adopted a black child against a matched sample of 41 white couples who had adopted a white child.[9] All of the families lived in Wisconsin. The two groups were matched on the age of the adopted child and on the socioeconomic status of the adoptive parent. All of the children in the study were preschoolers. The overall findings indicated that the outcomes of the transracial (TRA) placements were as successful as the in-racial (IRA) placements. And Zastrow commented,

One of the most notable findings is that TRA parents reported considerably fewer problems related to the care of the child have arisen than they anticipated prior to the adoption. . . . Many of the TRA couples mentioned that they became "color-blind" shortly after adopting; i.e., they stopped seeing the child as a black, and came to perceive the child as an individual who is a member of their family.[10]

When the parents were asked to rate their overall satisfaction with the adoptive experience, 99 percent of the TRA parents and 100 percent of the IRA parents checked "extremely satisfying" or "more satisfying than dissatisfying." And on another measure of satisfaction—one in which the parents rated their degree of satisfaction with certain aspects of their adoptive experience—out of a possible maximum of 98 points, the mean score of the TRA parents was 92.1 and of the IRA parents, 92.0.

Using a mail survey in 1981, William Feigelman and Arnold Silverman compared the adjustment of 56 black children adopted by white families against 97 white children adopted by white families.[11] The parents were asked to assess their child's overall adjustment and to indicate the frequency with which their child demonstrated emotional and physical problems. Silverman and Feigelman concluded that the child's age—not the transracial adoption—had the most significant impact on development and adjustment. The older the child, the greater the problems. They found no relationship between adjustment and racial identity.

W. M. Womak and W. Fulton's study of transracial adoptees and nonadopted black preschool children found no significant differences in racial attitudes between the two groups of children.[12]

In 1983, Ruth McRoy and Louis Zurcher reported the findings of their study of 30 black adolescents who had been transracially adopted and 30 black adolescents who had been adopted by black parents.[13] McRoy and Zurcher commented that 60 percent of the TRA parents "seemed to have taken a color-blind attitude to racial differences between the adoptee and family."[14] They described these families as living in predominantly white communities, and their adopted children as attending predominantly white schools. They reported that 20 percent of the transracial parents acknowledged the adoptees' racial identity and the need to provide black role models for them. Those parents enrolled their child into an integrated school, moved to a mixed neighborhood, or became members of a church located in the black community. Their children expressed an interest in contact with other blacks and often discussed racial identity issues with their parents and peers.

Another 20 percent of the transracial families had adopted several black children and acknowledged that their family was no longer white, but interracial. They enrolled their children in integrated schools. Racial discussions and confrontations in the home were common. The children were taught to emphasize their black racial heritage. When the parents were asked to "denote their children's racial background," 83 percent of the in-racial adoptive parents (black parents and black children) listed their child's background as black/black, and 17 percent as black/white. Among the white parents who adopted black children, 27 percent reported their child's racial background as black/black, 57 percent as black/white, and the other 16 percent as black/Mexican, Indian, Korean, or Latin American.

In the concluding chapter of their book, McRoy and Zurcher wrote,

> The transracial and inracial adoptees in the authors' study were physically healthy and exhibited typical adolescent relationships with their parents, siblings, teachers, and peers. Similarly, regardless of the race of their adoptive parents, they reflected positive feelings of self-regard.[15]

Throughout the book, the authors emphasized that the quality of parenting was more important than whether the black child had been in-racially or transracially adopted: "Most certainly, transracial adoptive parents experience some challenges different from inracial adoptive parents, but in this study, all of the parents successfully met the challenges."[16]

Though we discuss intercountry adoption in the next section of this chapter, we will mention here another study of adolescent transracial adoptees—this one of Korean adolescents who had been adopted by white families in the United States—in which D. S. Kim reported that the respondents had "little Korean identity," but had developed healthy self-concepts relative to other groups of adolescents.[17] Using a mail survey, Kim administered the Tennessee Self-concept Scale and a scale designed to measure adolescent socialization to 406 Korean children between the ages of 12 and 17.

In 1988, Joan Shireman and Penny Johnson described the results of their study involving 26 in-racial (black) and 26 transracial adoptive families in Chicago.[18] They reported very few differences between the two groups of eight-year-old adoptees. Using the Clark and Clark Doll Test (the same measures we used in our first study) to establish racial identity, 73 percent of the transracial adoptees identified themselves as black, compared to 80 percent for the in-racially adopted black children. Interestingly, although three-quarters of the families lived in white neighborhoods, 46 percent of the transracial adoptees named a black among their best friends. The authors concluded that 75 percent of the transracial adoptees and 80 percent of the in-racial adoptees appeared to be doing quite well. They also commented that the transracial adoptees had developed pride in being black and were comfortable in interaction with both black and white races. In a 1992 unpublished report, Karen Vroegh—a researcher in the Shireman and associates project—concluded,

The majority of the adopted adolescents, whether TRA or IRA (inracially adopted) were doing well. The rate and type of identified problems were similar to those found in the general population. Over 90 percent of the TRA parents thought transracial adoption was a good idea.[19]

In 1988, Richard Barth and Marian Berry reported that transracial placements were no more likely to disrupt than other types of adoptions.[20] The fact that transracial placements were as stable as other more traditional adoptive arrangements was reinforced by data presented in 1988 at a North American Council on Adoptable Children (NACAC) meeting on adoption disruption. There it was reported that the rate of adoption disruptions averaged about 15 percent. Disruptions, they reported, did not appear to be influenced by the adoptees' race or gender or the fact that they were placed as a sibling group. When examining adoptive parent characteristics, neither religion, race, marital status, length of time married, educational achievement, nor income seemed predictive of adoption disruption.

Even though the research by David Fanshel reported in *Far from the Reservation* was conducted more than 20 years ago, it still remains the definitive study of the experiences of transracially adopted Native American children, and is therefore worth noting.[21]

On the whole, Fanshel saw in the results of his study grounds for cautious optimism. In Table 4.2, we see that he divided his families into seven adjustment levels and distributed them according to the degree to which the parents reported that they believed their adopted child had made the adjustment described at each level.

The distribution shows that only 10 percent of the parents perceived their children's future adjustment as "guarded" (Level 5), and only one child was seen to have a "dim" (Level 6) future. In Fanshel's words,

More than fifty percent of the children were rated as showing relatively problem-free adjustments (Levels 1 and 2) and another twenty-five per-

Table 4.2   Level of Adjustment Perceived by White Parents of American Indian Children, 1972 Fanshel Study

Number	Percent	Description of Level
10	10	*Level One* (Child is making an excellent adjustment in all spheres—the outlook for his future adjustment is *excellent*.)
41	43	*Level Two*
24	25	*Level Three* (Child is making an adequate adjustment—his strengths outweigh the weaknesses he shows—the outlook for his future adjustment is *hopeful*.)
10	10	*Level Four*
10	10	*Level Five* (Child is making a mixed adjustment—generally the problems he faces are serious and the outlook for his future adjustment is *guarded*.)
1	1	*Level Six*
None	None	*Level Seven* (Child is making an extremely poor adjustment—the outlook for his future adjustment is *unpromising*.)

Source: David Fanshel, *Far from the Reservation: The Transracial Adoption of American Indian Children* (Metuchen, N.J.: Scarecrow Press, 1972), p. 280.

cent were rated as showing adequate adjustment with strengths outweighing weaknesses (Level 3). Another ten percent of the children were rated at Level 4—located midway between adjustments regarded as adequate and those viewed as guarded.[22]

Many of the parents acknowledged that difficulties lay ahead, and that they expected that those difficulties would surface when their children reached adolescence and adulthood. Many felt that the difficulties would be proportional to the "full-bloodedness" of their children, and that children who appeared less distinctively Indian would have less turbulent experiences. The existence of anxiety or lack of it therefore rested on the degree to which the children were of mixed blood.

In examining which social and demographic factors correlated best with the parents' perceptions of the child's adjustment, Fanshel found the strongest relationship between age and adjustment. The older the child at the time of initial placement, the more difficult the adjustment. Fanshel also discovered an association between age at placement and parental strictness, noting that, the older the child, the more strict the adoptive parents tended to be.

It is important to emphasize that all these impressions were based on the *parents'* responses to their children's adjustment over three different time periods. A professional evaluation of parental impressions (referred to as the "overall child adjustment rating") was the yardstick by which the children's adjustments were viewed, and it served as the basis of predictions for the future. At no time did Fanshel involve the children in attempting to predict future adjustments. The child's sex appeared minimally related to adjustment, boys being defined as slightly more problematic than girls. A family's social position was also related to the child's adjustment. The higher the family's status, the more difficulty the child seemed to experience, and therefore the more problematic her or his behavior. Fanshel explained this phenomenon by suggesting that parents of higher socioeconomic status set higher standards of behavior for their children, and thus have higher expectations of adoption. There was no relationship between the parents' religious affiliation or degree of religiousness and a child's adjustment.

In his conclusion, Fanshel addressed the issue of whether the transracial adoption of American Indian children should be encouraged. He described the costs involved in transracial adoption and concluded that adoption was cheaper than foster care or institutionalization. He established that the children were secure and loved in their adoptive homes. He found that the adoptive parents were happy and satisfied with their children. Nevertheless, in the end, he concluded that the decision as to whether the practice should or should not continue would be made on political grounds, and not on the basis of the quality of the adjustment that parents and children experienced.

To return to a point made in the opening paragraphs of this chapter, research findings show that transracial adoption is in a child's best interest. Transracial adoptees do not lose their racial identities, they do not appear to be racially unaware of who they are, and they do not display negative or indifferent racial attitudes about themselves. On the contrary, it appears that transracially placed children and their families have as high a success rate as all other adoptees and their families.

When given the opportunity to express their views on transracial adoption, most people—black and white—support it. For example, in January 1991, *CBS This Morning* reported the results of a poll it conducted that asked 975 adults the question "Should race be a factor in adoption?" Seventy percent of white Americans said no, and 71 percent of African Americans said no. These percentages are the same as those reported by Gallup in 1971 when it asked a national sample the same question.

At its Seventy-eighth Annual National Convention in 1987 and again in 1992, the NAACP adopted the following resolution:

WHEREAS, there are a number of black children for adoption; and WHEREAS, black children are among the most difficult to place in adopted homes; and WHEREAS, there is a policy, written and unwritten by many agencies to place black children only with black people; NOW THEREFORE, BE IT RESOLVED, that the NAACP sponsors and supports efforts and for legislation that will encourage policies that place black children for adoption without regard to race.[23]

Studies of Intercountry Adoptions

We saw in Chapter 1 that intercountry adoption (ICA) began primarily as a North American philanthropic response to the devastation of Europe that included thousands of orphaned children as a result of World War II. With the rebuilding of the European continent and the stabilization of its economy, the problem of orphaned children was basically solved. But a revitalized economy coupled with a reduction in Europe's male population—again as a result of World War II— resulted in an increase in the rate of childlessness. Western societies then turned toward Third World countries, with their high birthrates, as a solution to the dearth of healthy infants in the West.

Less empirical work has been done on families who have adopted children from abroad than on transracial adoptions within a given society (especially the United States). *Intercountry Adoptions,* a volume edited by Howard Altstein and Rita Simon in 1990, included chapters describing experiences with intercountry adoptions in seven societies: the United States, Canada, Germany, Norway, Holland, Denmark, and Israel.[24] Each chapter contained information based on empirical studies. The findings reported from some of those countries are summarized below.

United States

The results of studies of intercountry adoptees in the United States suggest that children who are adopted as infants make positive adjustments to their new environments.[25] The parents are eager to have the children perceive themselves as fully integrated members of the families. The parents make considerable efforts at maintaining a multi-ethnic environment in their homes: preparing special food, having cultural artifacts and books in the homes, establishing ties with other families who have children of that culture and with ethnic organizations.

Older children—especially those who had been abandoned, left on the streets, or institutionalized—present greater risks to adoptive parents. Of the 80 families involving 106 intercountry adoptees that formed the basis of another Simon–Altstein study, conducted in 1985, we found four families who reported serious problems with at least one of their adopted children.

In one of the families, the adopted son was six years old when he came to them from a country in Central America. (They also adopted a daughter with whom there were no problems.) The boy had lived in a war zone for most of his young life and had seen a lot of people killed. Neither he nor his adoptive parents know what happened to his birth mother or father. "N" had been seeing a psychiatrist for the three years preceding our study. His parents described him as hyperactive, subject to extreme mood swings, and immature. He had also been abusive to his younger sister. In his parents' view, a major difficulty of N's adjustment was that he had been forced to be an adult in his birth country; now, in his adoptive country, he had to learn to be a child. N had very negative feelings about his birth country and wanted to be identified as 100-percent American.

Another family who had adopted four siblings from an island in the Caribbean discovered that the oldest boy—a ten-year-old child—had been sexually assaulting his younger sisters and a brother. The boy himself had been sexually abused, first by his biological father and then by older boys in a children's home. In addition to being assaultive toward his younger siblings, the boy was handicapped by severe mental retardation.

In addition to the four dramatic cases, we found that many of the older children had scars that were likely to remain with them for a long time. But even in the most difficult of the cases, none of the parents considered disrupting the adoption.

Norway

Norway, Denmark, Israel, and to a lesser extent Holland share several important characteristics. Each has relatively small populations and few native-born infants available for adoption. The only source of healthy infants in any real numbers lies outside their countries' own borders. In most cases, to adopt in these societies means to adopt a foreign born. If this option is precluded, childlessness is the result.

Barbro Saetersdal and Monica Dalen reviewed some of the existing research on Norwegian intercountry adoptions and concluded that, although there were some initial adjustment problems (particularly with Indian and Vietnamese children), they tended for the most part to diminish over time.[26] Problems that did remain were in the area of language—not acquisition or usage, but the interaction between language development and conceptual learning. The latter difficulties were seen most sharply in educational environments.

Based on their data, Saetersdal and Dalen suggested that there may be an "intercountry adoption personality," which in their view is an adoptee who outwardly appears well adjusted and quite attached to her or his adopted family—perhaps too attached. These children, they report, are in fact anxious and insecure about their positions in Norwegian society. As adolescents, they keep a "low profile" and are afraid to take risks; although they have many friends, few are considered close. As in other situations described in the Saetersdal–Dalen investigation, whether these traits are related to the adoption itself or whether they result from pre-adoption experiences is difficult to trace. The authors felt that, as adults, these children run the risk of becoming marginal to Norwegian society.

Germany

Martin Textor reports that the great majority of foreign-born adoptees—constituting about 25 percent of all German adoptions—have made excellent adjustments both within their adoptive families and to their adopted country.[27] For example, Textor claims that, on critical indexes such as self-concept measures and disruption rates, the ICAs' acclimation to their environments seems highly satisfactory. Like the findings reported in the U.S. studies, German studies also show that adoption success is more likely the younger the child at the time of placements, and the shorter the time she or he has spent in an institution.

But important policy and ethical issues regarding intercountry adoption have arisen in Germany. Of particular concern is the basic issue of the "moral correctness" of intercountry adoption. The query is usually worded something like this: "Rather than fulfilling the desires of Western couples for parenthood with the Third World's abandoned and orphaned children, would the West's energies be more honestly and appropriately spent in encouraging family and children programs and policies that support the efforts of developing governments to keep their parentless children within their own societies?" Programs aimed at increasing day-care facilities, family planning, and economic opportunities for women—to name a few—could significantly reduce the numbers of children available for intercountry adoption into the West.

Another concern is the fact that about half of all intercountry adoptions into Germany are privately arranged. Many of these adoptions appear to border on the illegal, with money exchanged between the birth mother and prospective adopters, and with an incomplete filing of necessary documents.

Denmark

Between 1970 and 1990 there were about 10,000 intercountry adoptions in Denmark, and Korean children represented about half of all those adopted. Based on a national sample of 384 intercountry adoptees between the ages of 18 and 25, Mette Rorbech examined a number of variables germane to these children's integration into Danish society.[28] Indicating that about two-thirds of her sample arrived in Denmark after the age of three, Rorbech noted that practically all of them had various levels of native language development—a characteristic not too dissimilar from many of the intercountry adoptees into Norway. Although her overall conclusion is that intercountry adoption into Denmark has been quite successful, Rorbech found several areas where difficulties have arisen, particularly around education and employment. For example, 20 percent of the intercountry adoptees have not gone beyond the ninth or tenth "form" (grade). Of this group, half are unemployed, and the other half—according to Rorbech—are underemployed. Both, therefore, seem to be "at risk." As a consequence of this shortened period of education, a larger percentage than average no longer live with their parents. Additionally, 20–25 percent of these adoptees indicated they rarely see their adoptive families.

In terms of national identity, 70 percent do not think they are a "kind of an immigrant," and 90 percent reported feeling "mostly Danish."[29] Rorbech concluded that the Danish adoption policy has been successful. Most of the ICAs have been integrated into Danish society. They live like their nonadopted peers and they feel Danish. Only a minority experienced negative or positive differential treatment during their childhood.

Holland

Based on his work in the Netherlands, Rene Hoksbergen argues for a redirection of Western efforts away from providing Third World children to childless Western couples.[30] While presenting convincing data demonstrating positive adjustments to Dutch society by inter-country adoptees, Hoksbergen urges the West in general, and Holland in particular, to aid developing nations in promoting social and economic programs aimed at correcting the conditions contributing to family disorganization in their societies. Successful implementation of these programs would both strengthen family ties in developing nations and reduce, if not eliminate, the continuation of foreign adoption of their children. He also discusses the extent to which past traumatic experiences in the children's native countries are responsible for emotional distress and social maladjustment where they exist in the ICAs, or whether they are more likely to be caused by the children's failure to adjust satisfactorily to their adoptive environment, irrespective of pre-adoption experiences. Like others, Hoksbergen considers age at the time of adoption to be a crucial predictor of success.

Israel

Israel, like Holland and Norway, is a country where many adoptees were born in foreign lands.[31] It is also a country where the probability of adopting a native-born infant is infinitesimal. In 1988, only 115 native nonrelated children were adopted by Israeli couples, and about 3,000 Israeli couples were awaiting adoptable children—a very large figure given the size of the Israeli population. The ministry responsible for adoption services has all but abandoned these couples, leaving them to fend for themselves. The couples' only realistic option for a healthy infant is to explore the international adoption marketplace.

A consequence of this combination of a severe shortage of adoptable infants and a lack of involvement on the part of the appropriate ministry forces most potential Israeli adopters toward attempting privately arranged intercountry adoptions. Such a situation is quite precarious, however, in that Israeli law does not recognize private/independent adoptions, but only those made through sanctioned governmental agencies.

According to Eliezer Jaffe, the fact that Israeli law forbids private adoptions has invited the use of "less than legal methods" by many couples. In some cases, these methods make international headlines. For example, it seems that many infants adopted in Brazil by Israeli families were not legally free for adoption, but had either been bought or stolen from their birth parent(s)—by intermediaries—and presented as legally free.

Summary of Studies on Intercountry Adoptions

The accounts reported in the various countries demonstrate different experiences. But some generalizations hold. The broadest one concerns the age of the child. Older adoptees—and this includes children over 12 months old—pose more problems than younger adoptees. The older children's emotional and social adjustments are more difficult, their learning problems more complicated, their integration into the family harder to achieve. To some extent, these behaviors have been reported in studies of in-racial and in-cultural adoptions; but they are exacerbated when the older child comes from a different racial and ethnic background. The problems are further exacerbated if the child experienced trauma in her or his birth culture. And many of them did, as a result of desertion by one or both parents, as a consequence of living in a war zone or in an area of terrorist activities, or as a function of observing their mothers engage in prostitution.

The heterogeneity or homogeneity of the society into which the children are adopted also makes a difference. Saetersdal and Dalen have argued that Norway is too homogeneous a society in which to socialize Asian, African, or any children who are non-Caucasian. To a lesser extent, Rorbech has made a similar observation about Denmark. The adoptees stand out too sharply, and their physical differences induce insecurity, fear, and denial on their part, which in turn results in poor school performance and poor overall adjustment.

Hoksbergen is one of the leaders among adoption researchers who have advocated long-distance sponsorship as an alternative to adoption. He has expressed ambivalence about transporting children out of their native cultures into Western societies, and has advocated policies that would keep the children in the homeland of their birth parents, with institutional supports that would provide them with educational opportunities, economic security, and emotional ties. Hoksbergen's views on establishing systems whereby children are supported and maintained in their birth culture has allies in Germany and other parts of Europe. Martin Textor in writing about Germany, for example, has observed that in (what was) West Germany the families' motivations for ICA are more altruistic, stemming more from a sense of noblesse oblige than they do in the United States where the desire to parent a child is the uppermost consideration.

The major finding that emerges from these cases studies is the variation that exists across societies. One should not generalize from the experiences of any one of them. While the age of the child may be important in each of them, how that variable interacts with the motivations of the adoptive families, with the homogeneity or heterogeneity of the adoptive society, and with the attitudes of the adoptive society to the ethnic and racial backgrounds of the adoptive children produces sufficiently different scenarios—making it difficult to predict how successful intercountry adoptions are likely to be as an overall strategy for helping homeless and parentless children in Third World countries. The bottom-line question that one should always ask is whether these children would be better off in their birth countries—in institutions, foster care, or even adopted—than they would be in the United States or Western Europe.

Notes

1. Lucille J. Grow and Deborah Shapiro, *Black Children, White Parents: A Study of Transracial Adoption* (New York: Child Welfare League of America, 1974).

2. Ibid., p. ii.

3. Ibid., p. 89.

4. Ibid., p. 90.

5. Joyce Ladner, *Mixed Families* (New York: Archer Press, Doubleday, 1977).

6. Ibid., pp. xii–xiii.

7. Ibid., p. 254.

8. Ibid., pp. 255–56.

9. Charles H. Zastrow, *Outcome of Black Children–White Parents Transracial Adoptions* (San Francisco: R&E Research Associates, 1977).

10. Ibid., p. 81.

11. William Feigelman and Arnold Silverman, *Chosen Child: New Patterns of Adoptive Relationships* (New York: Praeger, 1983).

12. Womack and Fulton, "Transracial Adoption and the Black Preschool Child," 20 *Journal American Academy of Child Psychiatry* 712–24 (1981).

13. Ruth McRoy and Louis A. Zurcher, *Transracial and Inracial Adoptees* (Springfield, Ill.: Charles C. Thomas, 1983).

14. Ibid., p. 130.

15. Ibid., p. 138.

16. Ibid., p. 138.

17. D. S. Kim, "Intercountry Adoptions: A Study of Self-concept of Adolescent Korean Children Who Were Adopted by American Families," unpublished Ph.D. thesis, University of Chicago, 1976.

18. Joan Shireman and Penny Johnson, *Growing Up Adopted* (Chicago: Chicago Child Care Society, 1988).

19. Karen Vroegh, "Transracial Adoption: How It Is 17 Years Later," unpublished report, Chicago Child Care Society, Chicago, April 1992.

20. Richard P. Barth and Marian Berry, *Adoption and Disruption* (New York: Aldine de Gruyter, 1988), pp. 3–35.

21. David Fanshel, *Far from the Reservation: The Transracial Adoption of American Indian Children* (Metuchen, N.J.: Scarecrow Press, 1972).

22. Ibid., p. 280.

23. National Association for the Advancement of Colored People, resolution of the Seventy-eighth Annual National Convention, Washington, D.C., 1987.

24. Howard Altstein and Rita J. Simon, eds., *Intercountry Adoption* (New York, Praeger, 1991).

25. Rita J. Simon and Howard Altstein, "Intercountry Adoptions: Experiences of Families in the United States," in Altstein and Simon, *Intercountry Adoption*.

26. Barbro Saetersdal and Monica Dalen, "Intercountry Adoptions in a Homogeneous Country," in Altstein and Simon, *Intercountry Adoption*.

27. Martin Textor, "International Adoption in West Germany: A Private Affair," in Altstein and Simon, *Intercountry Adoption*.

28. Mette Rorbech, "The Conditions of 18 and 25 Year Old Foreign-born Adoptees in Denmark," in Altstein and Simon, *Intercountry Adoption*.

29. Unlike Norway and Sweden—neighboring countries that register intercountry adoptees as "immigrant"—Denmark registers such newcomers as Danish nationals from the moment they arrive.

30. Rene Hoksbergen, "Intercountry Adoption Coming of Age in the Netherlands," in Altstein and Simon, *Intercountry Adoption*.

31. Eliezer Jaffe, "Foreign Adoptions in Israel: Private Paths to Parenthood," in Altstein and Simon, *Intercountry Adoption*.

5

The Simon–Altstein 20-Year Study of Transracial Adoption

The results of the first of the Simon–Altstein studies appeared in 1977.[1] In 1992, *Adoption, Race, and Identity* reported the findings of three of the surveys, thereby including all of the work that had been done up through 1984.[2] This chapter summarizes the findings of those first three surveys, which covered a 13-year time span, and then reports in more detail the results of the last survey conducted in 1990–91. Those findings appear here for the first time in print.

Research Design and Sample Frame

In 1971–72, Rita Simon contacted 206 families living in five cities in the Midwest who were members of the Open Door Society and the Council on Adoptable Children (COAC) and asked them whether she could interview them about their decision to adopt a nonwhite child. All of the families but two (who declined for reasons unrelated to adoption) agreed to participate in the study. The parents allowed a two-person team composed of one male and one female graduate student to interview them in their home for 60–90 minutes at the same time that each of their children, who were between four and eight years old, was being interviewed for about 30 minutes. In total, 204 parents and 366 children were interviewed.

Seven years later, Rita Simon and Howard Altstein sought out these families again and were able to locate 71 percent of them. The remaining 29 percent of the families were unreachable through any of the channels we tried. We contacted local chapters of the Open Door Society and COAC officers and consulted membership lists of various other transracial adoption organizations. We asked for information from people who had helped us seven years before. All of our leads in these cases resulted in returned "undeliverable" envelopes. While it is unfortunate that we were unable to locate all of the original families, we were gratified that we could reach 71 percent of them seven years later. Of the families we did reach, 93 percent agreed to participate in the second survey. Ten of the 143 families did not. The interviews at that time—which were done only with the parents, and by mail or phone—focused on their relations with their adopted child(ren) and on the children born to them, on the children's racial identity, and on the ties that both the adopted and the nonadopted children had to their larger family units (i.e., grandparents, aunts, and uncles), their schools, and their communities.

In the fall of 1983 and the winter of 1984, the families were contacted a third time. We returned to our original design and conducted personal interviews in the respondents' homes, with both the parents and the adolescent children.

Of the 133 families who participated in the 1979 study, 88 took part in the 1984 survey. In addition, eight families who had participated in the 1971 study, but could not be found in 1979, were located in 1984 and participated. From among the 133 families who had been involved in the 1979 study, 28 had moved and could not be located; or in a few cases, when we did find them, we could not arrange to interview them. In one family, the only child who was transracially adopted had died in an auto accident. Eleven families declined to be interviewed; and in one city, the interviewing team did not complete the scheduled interviews, and we thereby lost five families. The refusal rate of 10 percent—while still low—was slightly higher than the 7 percent we received in 1979. Among the 11 families who did not wish to be interviewed, two had been divorced since 1979. The family members were separated, and some of them did not wish to "get involved." Three families had been interviewed by other researchers and felt that "enough is enough." The members of one family said that they had gone through a number of family problems recently and that this was not a good time for them. The other five families gave no reason.

Going back to the 1979 profiles of the 11 families who declined to be interviewed in 1983–84, we found that in five of the families the parents described problems between themselves and their children. These problems included the following: the child had a "learning disability that put a lot of stress on the family"; the child was "hyperactive and was experiencing identity problems"; the child was "retarded and was having personality problems''; the child had "a severe learning disability and behavioral problems that [affected] school performance''; "the adoption has not been accepted by the extended family." Another set of parents, who characterized their relations with their transracially adopted child as "negative," traced the problems to a brain injury that had resulted from an automobile accident.

In five families, the parents agreed to be interviewed but—for a variety of reasons—did not allow their children to participate. Among the reasons given were the following: only the transracially adopted children were still at home, and the parents felt that they were too young (14 and 15 years old) to go through an interview that probed into the areas we were covering; the children did not seem interested, and the parents did not want to pressure them; and, in one family, the only child still at home stated specifically that she did not want to be interviewed.

In total, the 96 families had 394 children, consisting of 213 boys and 181 girls; 256 were still living at home, and 34 were away at school but considered the parents' home their home. The others had moved away, were working, or were married. Forty-three percent of all the children had been transracially adopted.

We interviewed 218 children. They represented 55 percent of the total number of children born to or adopted by the parents and 85 percent of the children still living at home. Of the 34 children who were attending colleges or universities and considered their parents' home their official residence, we were able to interview a few when they were home on vacation. Some of the children remaining at home were too young (not yet adolescents) to be included in this phase of the study. Fifty-four percent of those at home were transracially adopted. Among the transracial adoptees (TRAs), we interviewed 61 boys and 50 girls, or 80 percent of those at home. Eighty-nine of the 111 TRAs were American black. The others were Korean, Native American, Eskimo, or Vietnamese. We also interviewed 48 males and 43 females who were born into the families and four males and 12 females who are white adoptees.

The median ages of the children interviewed in the three categories were 14.9 years for the TRAs, 16.8 years for those born to the parents, and 16.9 for the same-race adoptees. Their ordinal positions in the family are shown in Table 5.1.

The third survey focused on how the family members related to each other, the racial identities of the adopted children, the adopted children's sense of integration with their families, and the parents' and

Table 5.1   Children's Ordinal Position in Their Families, Simon–Altstein Third Survey, 1983–84

Position	TRA	Born (percent)	White Adoptee
Only child	1.0	—	—
Oldest child	7.2	35.1	31.3
Middle child	10.8	15.4	12.5
Youngest child	47.7	12.1	6.3
Other position	33.3	37.4	49.9
Total	100 (111)	100 (91)	100 (16)

children's expectations concerning the children's future identity. We asked about the bonds that the TRAs were likely to have toward the mainly white-oriented world of their parents and siblings, and the ties that the TRAs were likely to develop with the community of their racial and ethnic backgrounds, or with some composite world.

The fourth phase of the study began in 1991. We were able to locate 83 of the 96 families who had participated in the 1984 study. Of those 83 families, 76 (92 percent) provided us with the names and addresses of their adult transracially adopted and birth children. Seven families opted not to participate. In 1993, we reviewed the interviews we had conducted with those seven families and found nothing unusual in them. One set of parents had divorced in 1974: the two children—one adopted and one birth child—were living with the mother; the father saw them on weekends and holidays. The parents and children in the other six families were all intact. The children were attending universities or high schools. There was no mention by the parents or the children of physical or emotional/mental illnesses, or of drug or alcohol use. Those families who offered an explanation for their unwillingness to participate said their children "weren't particularly interested," or that "they had a busy schedule and did not want to take the time." Of the remaining 76 families, four had children who were still in high school, and we chose not to interview them.

This last phase focused almost exclusively on the adult children. Brief telephone interviews were conducted with their parents—mostly to ask them whether, with the knowledge of more than 20 years of hindsight, they would have done what they did, that is, adopt across racial lines; and whether they would advise families like themselves, today, to adopt a child of a different race. But the long in-depth personal interviews were conducted only with the children. We asked them to talk about their experiences growing up in an unusual family environment—to assess how their family situation affected their social and racial identities, their racial attitudes, and their sense of awareness about racial issues. Many of these themes were explored in the earlier phases of the study. But now the children were young adults, and we wanted them to reflect and comment on their experiences.

We asked the children to describe how they felt about being the only black (or Korean, etc.) person in their family—how it affected their overall personality, their sense of security and their identity. What would they have wanted their parents to have done differently? For example, would they have wanted them to have moved into mixed racial neighborhoods rather than continue to live in the predominantly white neighborhoods in which most of the families resided? Were there other aspects of their family life—for example, the churches they attended, the friends the family had, the relations they maintained with grandparents, aunts, and uncles, or the groups and organizations with which they were involved—that they would have wanted their parents to have changed? Would they have wanted their parents and siblings to have interacted differently with them?

We asked them about their education, the work they were doing, the amount of money they were earning, and whether they were married and had a family. We asked them to describe their close friends and the type of community in which they were living. When did they leave their parents' home, and what were the circumstances under which they left? Did they now perceive themselves as integral members of their family? For example, we asked how much time they now spent with their parents and siblings. How much of their lives did they now share with them? What efforts, if any, had they expended on locating their birth parents? If they did seek out one or both birth parents, what motivated them to do so, and how successful were they in locating them?

Major Findings

Parent Socioeconomic Characteristics

When we examined the parents' responses to the initial interview schedule in 1972, we were struck by the homogeneity of the families' social and economic status. Their educational backgrounds, for example, showed that at least 62 percent of the mothers had completed four years of college and 28 percent of them had continued on to graduate school. Sixty-one percent of the fathers had attended university past the bachelor's degree. Another 18 percent had completed at least four years of college. Sixty-eight percent of the fathers worked as professionals. Most of them were ministers, social workers, or academicians. Among the remaining third, 12 percent were businessmen, and the other 20 percent were clerical workers, salesmen, skilled laborers, or graduate students.

None of the mothers held full-time jobs outside their homes. Almost all of them explained that, when they and their husbands made the decision to adopt, this also involved a commitment on the wife's part to remain at home in the role of full-time mother. Before they were married, or before they adopted their first child, 46 percent of the mothers had held jobs in a professional capacity, and 3 percent had been enrolled as graduate students. About 14 percent did not work outside the home before they gave birth to, or adopted, their first child. The parents' median income in 1972 was $16,500.

The average age of the mother was 34, and that of the father, 36. The range for both parents in 1972 was between 25 and 50. They had been married for an average of 12 years; the shortest time was two years and the longest was 25 years.

The Midwest is heavily Protestant, and so were the respondents in our sample. Sixty-three percent of the mothers and 57 of the fathers acknowledged belonging to some Protestant congregation. Lutheranism was cited by 19 percent of both mothers and fathers. Twenty-one percent of the mothers and 22 percent of the fathers were Catholics, 1 and 2 percent were Jewish, and the remaining 15 and 19 percent acknowledged no formal religious identification or affiliation. Most of the parents who acknowledged a religious affiliation also said they attended church regularly, at least once a week. The church played an important role in the lives of many of these families. Some reported that much of their social life was organized around their church, and that many their friends belonged to it—especially other families who had adopted nonwhite children.

Political affiliations and activities were not as important as the church for most of the families. About a third of the parents described themselves as independents, about 40 percent as Democrats, and 12 percent as Republicans; the others had no preference or named a local party (in Minnesota, the Farmer Labor party) as the one they generally supported or had voted for in the previous election. Only a small proportion—less than a quarter of the group—said that they belonged to a local political club or that they worked for a political candidate.

The socioeconomic characteristics of the families in our study closely matched those reported by Lucille Grow and Deborah Shapiro.[3] Although Grow and Shapiro's families were distributed across all regions of the United States, they found—as we did—that the parents were better educated than average (a majority of the fathers having attended university past the bachelor's degree, and about half of the mothers having attended college for at least four years). More than half of the fathers held professional or technical positions. They also found that about two-thirds of the families were Protestant and that most of the parents were regular churchgoers. Religion played an important part in the lives of the families in the Grow and Shapiro sample, as it did in ours. Many of their respondents, like ours, traced their motivation for adopting a nonwhite child to their religious beliefs and church affiliation.

In both samples, the parents thought of themselves as liberals or independents, but—with few exceptions (10 and 4 percent, respectively)—the families lived in all-white or predominantly white neighborhoods. In other words, although in both surveys the parents claimed to be more liberal in their political views or affiliations than their socioeconomic status might lead one to predict, their choice of where to live was quite consistent with their status as middle-class, educated, professional people.

Birth and Adoption Patterns

The number of children per family in our surveys ranged from one to seven; this included birth as well as adopted children. Nineteen percent of the parents did not have any birth children. All of those families reported that they were unable to bear children. The range of children born and adopted in all the families is shown in Table 5.2.

The families who adopted more than three children were in almost all instances ones in which the father or both parents were professionally involved in adoption services, youth work, or social work. They had prior experience as foster parents, and some had foster children currently living with them. In a sense, their decision to adopt and their plans to make themselves available as foster parents were part of their professional roles.

Twenty-six percent of the families adopted their first child. Since 19

Table 5.2   Total Number of Children, Number Adopted, and Number Born into Families, Simon–Altstein Surveys, 1971–91

Total Number of Children	Percentage of Families		Number of Children Adopted	Number of Children Born into Family
1	3	3	1	—
2	16		1	1
2	10	26	2	—
3	2		3	—
3	6		2	1
3	18	26	1	2
4	3		4	—
4	2		3	1
4	9		2	2
4	10	24	2	2
5	1		5	—
5	1		4	1
5	1		3	2
5	4		2	3
5	4	11	1	4
6	1		4	2
6	1		2	4
6	2	4	1	5
7	2		4	3
7	2		2	5
7	1	5	1	6

percent of these parents were unable to bear children, it turns out that only 7 percent of those who had children born to them had adopted their first child. In many cases, the fact that parents who were not infertile had children born to them before they adopted was not a matter of choice, but a reflection of the policy of the adoption agency with which they were dealing. Unless a couple could produce medical evidence that they were unable to bear a child, most of them were "strongly advised" to have at least one child; and then, if they were still interested in adoption, the agency would be willing to consider their candidacy.

Twenty-six percent of the time, the first adopted child was the oldest child in the family; 32 percent of the time, she or he was the middle child; and 41 percent of the time, he or she was the youngest child. Among those families who adopted more than one child (56 percent), the second adopted child occupied the "middle" position 35 percent of the time and the "youngest" position 65 percent of the time. American blacks made up the largest category of adopted children. They also comprised the category of children who were the most available for adoption. Table 5.3 describes the racial, sexual, and adoptive statuses of the children in the study.

Most of the families wanted a racially mixed child, but they did not have strong preferences concerning the specific characteristics of the mixture. Some of the families—but fewer than ten—said they felt that the problems of adopting a black child would be more than they were willing or able to undertake. One family said, "At the time we weren't ready to adopt a black child. Taking an Indian child was less of a step."

A member of another family said about the adoption experience, "I was afraid of what my parents and other people would say. But I've changed and, by the time we adopted our second child, I only wanted a Negro child."

Comments such as the above also came from parents who adopted Korean or American Indian children. But more typical responses were ones such as the following:

We wanted more children than two. We started worrying about the population explosion. We knew that there was not much of a possibility of our adopting a white child. We felt that we could handle a child that maybe some other people could not. We knew that there was a need for parents who would adopt a racially mixed child. Once we decided to adopt, we discussed who we would like to adopt and we both agreed that

Table 5.3 Racial, Sexual, and Adoptive Statuses of Children Subjects, Simon–Altstein Surveys, 1971–91

	Adoptive Status				
	Adopted		Born to Family		
Racial Background	Boys	Girls	Boys	Girls	Total
White	21	21	100	67	209
Black	75	45	—	—	120
American Indian, Asian, etc.	16	21	—	—	37
Total	112	87	100	67	366

we'd like to adopt a minority child. I think part of the reason was that we had both spent two years in Africa in the Peace Corps. Seeing all these differences in people was interesting and exciting and not threatening. And we wanted to, if we could, incorporate those differences into our family. So we decided we would take a minority child and we weren't really specific as to what kind. We didn't think in terms of a black child or Indian child. We just thought whoever needed a home we would take. At the time, the hardest to place child was the black child, and so since we had been in Africa, that was no problem with us. We had some black friends with whom we were fairly close and we decided that was fine. We wanted any mixed race, Negro or Indian, any mixed race. We told the agency it made no difference as long as she is brown.

The members of one family who adopted a black child felt that they had been propagandized and given misinformation by the adoption agency. Mrs. "G." said,

We were all naive about our racial feelings. We wanted to do good works. We had all this input from agencies who said that no black families would adopt. We gained the impression that the children would stay in institutions for the rest of their lives. We believed that these agencies knew the truth and were telling it to us. Since we wanted to have a different kind of family, one with all kinds of people in it and since we thought we could provide a good home and since we were interested in black people and black culture and since we had a feeling that we wanted to know more about black people and what their struggle was, we went about with the adoption.

Mr. and Mrs. G. felt that the agencies had deceived them, and that indeed there are black parents who want to adopt black children: "We feel now that if a black child can find a black home, that is the ideal. If we were to adopt today, knowing what we know about the interest and availability of black parents, we would not adopt a black child and we would not help or advise anyone else to do it."

Among those families who adopted one child, 56 percent adopted a boy, and 44 percent a girl. Among those families who adopted more than one child, 60 percent adopted boys and girls, 22 percent adopted only boys, and 18 percent adopted only girls. The sex ratio for all the adopted children shows that 41 percent of the families adopted only a boy, 32 percent adopted only a girl, and 27 percent adopted both sexes. The overall pattern thus reveals a slight preference for boys over girls. In almost every instance, when parents expressed a preference for a boy or girl, it was because they wanted a child to match or complement a desired family pattern. For some, a girl was needed as a sister, or a boy was wanted as a brother; for others, there were only boys in the family, and the parents wanted a daughter, or vice versa. In only a few instances did childless parents indicate that they had a sex preference.

The ages at which the first and second children were adopted are shown in Table 5.4. Note that 69 percent of the first-child adoptions were of children less than one year of age, compared to 80 percent of the second-child adoptions. One explanation for the greater proportion of younger adoptions the second time around is that adoption agencies were more likely to provide such families—who had already proven themselves by their successful first adoption—with their most desirable and sought-after children, than they were to place such children in untried homes.

In 1972, only a minority of the families we contacted had considered adopting a nonwhite child initially. Most of them said they had wanted a healthy baby. When they found that they could not have a healthy *white* baby, they sought to adopt a healthy black, Indian, or Korean baby—rather than an older white child or a physically or mentally handicapped white child or baby. They preferred a child of another race to a child whose physical or mental handicaps might cause considerable financial drain or emotional strain. About 40 percent of the families intended or wanted to adopt nonwhite children because of their own involvement in the civil rights movement and as a reflection of their general sociopolitical views. Eighty-one percent of the families had at least one child born to them before they adopted transracially. In many instances, the adoption agency told them to "come back" after they had borne a child.

Table 5.4   Ages of Children at First and Second Adoption, Simon–Altstein Surveys, 1971–91

Ages	First Adoption	Second Adoption
	(in percent)	
Less than 1 month	11	11
1–2 months	27	24
3–5 months	13	28
6–11 months	18	17
1 year–1 year 11 months	11	10
2 years–2 years 11 months	3	1
3 years–4 years 11 months	6	2
5 years and older	8	7
No answer	2	—

In summary, the demographic characteristics for the first survey show that, on the average, families had between three and four children. Forty-four percent adopted one child, and 41 percent adopted two children. The large majority adopted after they had borne at least one child (although not necessarily as a matter of choice). Black children were adopted by at least two-thirds of the families, followed by Native American, Korean, white, and Mexican or Puerto Rican children. When a family adopted one child, there was a slightly greater likelihood that it would be a boy; but when more than one child was adopted, 60 percent adopted both a boy and a girl. About 70 percent of the first adoptions and 80 percent of the second adoptions were of babies less than one year old.

Of the families that we contacted seven years later, at least a third of the mothers were working full-time outside their homes. For some of them, it was a matter of necessity; for others, it was a matter of choice. Among the women who returned to work by choice, almost all were engaged in professional positions of the type they had left before they adopted their first child. The women who worked out of necessity were divorced and had become the heads of their households. Most held white-collar or secretarial jobs. The majority of the women in the survey chose to remain at home as full-time housewives and mothers.

In 1972, all the families were intact: there were no separations, divorces, or deaths. By 1979, two of the fathers had died. In one family, both parents died, and the older siblings were raising the younger ones. In one family, the parents were separated; and in 19 families, the parents were divorced. In three of those 19, the father had custody of the children.

Twenty-three families adopted one more child after 1972, and 12 families had another child born to them. Of the children adopted after 1972, five were white, 11 were American black, and the other seven were Vietnamese refugees. Thirteen were boys and ten were girls. Eighteen percent of the parents reported that at least one child had left home to attend college or to marry.

Neighborhoods, Schools, and Friends

In 1972, 78 percent of the survey families were living in all-white neighborhoods. Four percent lived in predominantly black neighborhoods, and the other 18 percent lived in mixed neighborhoods. Among the large majority who lived in all-white neighborhoods, only a few said they planned to move when their adopted children approached school age. Most of the parents saw no incongruity between their family composition and their choice of neighborhood.

Little changed in that respect over the years. In 1979, 77 percent of the families were still living in all-white or predominantly white neighborhoods. The others lived in mixed communities. Several families who lived in white neighborhoods transferred their church memberships to mixed congregations in other neighborhoods. One mother said, "We did this chiefly to give our adopted daughter greater personal acceptance and support there also."

A few of the families who lived in mixed neighborhoods moved there because they wanted a better racial mix for their children. One parent in a mixed neighborhood reported that, of the eight families on their block, four had adopted transracially. Several parents said that they planned to move into a mixed community before their adopted children became teenagers.

On the other hand, one parent said that his family had decided to leave a mixed neighborhood because their children were making such observations as, "All blacks steal," and "Most black kids get into trouble with the police." The mixed neighborhood was less affluent than the one in which they had lived previously.

Seventy-one percent of the parents reported that their children attended mixed schools, and 6 percent said the schools were mostly black. With one exception, all the children in this latter category lived with their mothers after their parents had divorced. A lower standard of living seemed to be the major factor for the child's attending a predominantly black school, as opposed to a different ideological position or commitment.

Eighty-eight percent of both the fathers and mothers participated in the 1983–84 study. Among the remaining 12 percent, the mother served as the respondent most of the time. Returning to the families four and a half years after our second study, we found that 83 percent of the parents were still married to their original partners; six had divorced before 1979, and two after 1979. Three pairs of parents were separated. Half of the divorced couples had remarried. The mother had custody of the children in four families; the father, in two. There was joint custody in two, and each parent had custody of at least one child in three families. In four of the families, the father died; and in one family, both parents died before 1979 and the children were being reared by older siblings.

In 1984, 72 percent of the mothers were employed full-time outside their homes, almost all of them in technical and white-collar positions as teachers, nurses, and secretaries. Sixty-six percent of the fathers continued to work in professional fields as lawyers, ministers, teachers, professors, and doctors. Most of the others were in business. The median family income was $44,000.

The strength and form of the families' religious attachments remained much the same as they had been in earlier years. Of the 80 percent who designated a religious preference, 19 percent were Catholics, 2 percent were Jews, and the others were Protestants, with Lutheranism named most often by those who reported a religious preference. Fifty-two percent said that they attended church at least once a week. Forty-eight percent of the mothers and 46 percent of the fathers said that they preferred the Democratic over the Republican party; 53 percent of the mothers and 48 percent of the fathers described themselves as "liberals," as opposed to 8 and 16 percent, respectively, who labeled themselves "conservatives."

Ninety-three percent of the families lived in single-dwelling homes in residential neighborhoods. Seventy-three percent of the parents described their neighborhood as completely or almost completely white. Eighty percent of the parents reported that they had been living in the same house for at least ten years.

In 1983–84, the TRAs were most likely to be the youngest children still at home—81 percent of them, compared to 17 percent of the children born into the family and 1 percent of the white adoptees. All but four of the TRAs were still in school at the time of the study; 15 of the children born to the families and four of the white adoptees were no longer in school.

Among the children at the precollege level, 83 percent of the TRAs, 82 percent of those born into the family, and 80 percent of the white adoptees were attending public institutions. At the college level as well, most of the children were attending public universities, with no differences from one adopted status to another.

The racial composition of the schools that the children attended were described by them as follows:

76–100 percent white	58
51–75 percent white	22
50-percent white	10
Less than 50-percent white	10

The birth children and the white adoptees were no more likely to have attended the predominantly white schools than were the transracially adopted children.

In 1990–91, 24 percent of the TRAs and 63 percent of the birth children had thus far completed at least a baccalaureate degree. All but 10 percent of the TRAs said that they planned to go on with their schooling for at least a baccalaureate degree or higher. Among those currently attending colleges or universities, about 60 percent of their parents, or their parents plus tuition scholarships, were paying for tuition, room, and board—for both the TRAs and the birth children.

Forty percent of the birth children and 13 percent of the TRAs were currently married. Of the 12 married birth children, two of their spouses were Asian; among the TRAs, one out of five of the black adopted children was married to a black person, and the other four had white spouses.

Of the TRAs who were currently employed (84 percent), 18 percent were professionals; 20 percent worked in administrative or clerical jobs, and 43 percent in skilled and services jobs; the others were in the armed services or doing other things. All but 3 percent of the birth children were employed—one-third in professional work, one-third in administrative or clerical positions, 17 percent in skilled and services jobs, and 13 percent in other positions.

Sixty percent of the TRAs and 77 percent of the birth children lived in neighborhoods that were mostly white. Fifty-eight percent of the TRAs and 57 percent of the birth children attended the same church as their parents.

The Adoption Experience

The most important finding that emerged from our first encounter with the families in 1971–72 was the absence of a white racial preference or bias on the part of the white birth children and the nonwhite adopted children. Contrary to other findings that had been reported up to that time, the children reared in these homes appeared indifferent to the advantages of being white, but aware of and comfortable with the racial identity imposed on them by their outward appearance. By and large, the parents of these children were confident that the atmosphere, the relationships, the values, and the lifestyle to which the children were being exposed would enable successful personal adjustments as adults. In writing about the results of our study in 1977,

Simon and Altstein emphasized that transracial adoption appeared to provide the opportunity for children to develop an awareness of race, a respect for the physical differences imposed by race, and an ease with their own racial characteristics, whatever they may be.

When we returned to these families in 1979, we learned that the "extremely glowing, happy portrait" that we had painted seven years earlier now had some blemishes on it. It showed signs of stress and tension. We noted that

> for every five families in which there were the usual pleasures and joys along with sibling rivalries, school-related problems, and difficulties in communication between parent and child, there was one family whose difficulties were more profound and were believed by the parents to have been directly related to the transracial adoption.[4]

The serious problem most frequently cited by the parents was the adopted child's (usually a boy's), tendency to steal from other members of the family. We described parents' accounts of the theft of bicycles, clothing, stereos, and money from siblings' rooms, to the point where brothers and sisters had resorted to putting locks on their bedroom doors. Another serious problem was certain parents' rather painful discovery that their adopted children had physical, mental, or emotional disabilities—either genetic or the result of indifferent or abusive treatment received in foster homes.

Our third survey encounter occurred in 1983–84 when most of the children were adolescents. We found that almost all of the families had made some changes in their lives. Most of the time, however, the changes were not made because they had decided to adopt a child of a different race, but because the adoption added another child to the family. Thus, the parents talked about buying a bigger house, adding more bedroom space, having less money for vacations and entertainment, and allowing less time for themselves. In retrospect, most of the parents did not dwell on what they wished they had done but did not do; nor did they berate themselves for things they did and wished they had not done. Most of them felt that they were doing their best. They worked hard at being parents, and at being parents of children of a different race.

In the early years, many of them were enthusiastic about introducing the culture of the TRA's background into the family's day-to-day life. This was especially true of the families who had adopted Native American and Korean children. They experimented with new recipes;

sought out books, music, and artifacts; joined churches and social organizations; traveled to the Southwest for ethnic ceremonies; and participated in local ethnic events. The parents of black children primarily introduced books about black history and black heroes, joined a black church, sought out black playmates for their children, and celebrated Martin Luther King's birthday. In a few families, a black friend became the godparent to their transracially adopted child. One mother told us, "Black parents regard us as black parents."

But as the years wore on, as the children became teenagers and pursued their own activities and social life, the parents' enthusiasm and interest for "ethnic variety" waned. An increasing number of families lived as their middle-class and upper-middle-class white neighbors did. Had the children shown more interest—more desire to maintain ethnic contacts and ties—most of the parents said they would have been willing to follow the same direction. In the absence of signals that the activities were meaningful to their children, the parents decided that the one-culture family was an easier route.

Karen Vroegh of the Shireman and associates study in Chicago (see Chapter 4) reported that "more TRA than IRA [interracial adoption] parents mentioned activities they thought might help their teenagers assume a black identity. Some lived in multiracial neighborhoods and others had black friends and attended church among blacks."[5]

Almost all of the parents in our study said that they were affected by the stance taken by the National Association of Black Social Workers and that of the Native American councils in the 1970s vis-à-vis the adoption of black and Native American children by white families. Almost all of the survey parents thought that the position taken by those groups was contrary to the best interest of the child and smacked of racism. They were angered by the accusations of the NABSW that white parents could not rear black children, and they felt betrayed by groups whose respect they expected they would have. Race, they believed, was not and should not be an important criterion for deciding a child's placement. In their willingness to adopt, they were acting in the best interest of a homeless, neglected, unwanted child. One parent said, "Our children are the ones no one wanted. Now they are saying you are the wrong family."

In the 1983–84 phase, all of the children in the study were asked to complete a "self-esteem scale," which in essence measures how much respect a respondent has for herself or himself. A person is characterized as having high self-esteem if she or he considers herself or himself to be a person of worth. Low self-esteem means that the individual lacks self-respect. Because we wanted to make the best possible comparison among our respondents, we examined the scores of our black TRAs separately from those of the other TRAs and from those of the white born and white adopted children. The scores for all four groups were virtually the same. No one group of respondents manifested higher or lower self-esteem than the others. The Shireman and associates study also included the self-esteem scale, and they report that "the majority of the teenage adoptees . . . whether TRA or IRA, black or mixed, have good self-esteem."[6]

The lack of difference among our respondents on the self-esteem scale reminds us of the lack of difference we reported for these children in the first study when we asked them to choose dolls of different races. The scores obtained demonstrated that none of the children manifested a white racial preference.

We wrote about these findings in our first volume as follows:

> There was no consistent preference for the white doll among the black, white, and Indian or Oriental children. There was no indication that the black children had acquired racial awareness earlier than the white children, and there was no evidence that the white children were able to identify themselves more accurately than the non-white children.[7]

Our 1977 study was the first to report that there were no white racial preferences among American black and white children. The responses suggested that the unusual family environment in which these children were being reared might have caused their deviant racial attitudes and resulted in their not sharing with other American children a sense that white is preferable to other races. We noted that the children's responses also demonstrated that their deviant racial attitudes did not affect their ability to identify themselves accurately.

The lack of differences among our adolescent responses was again dramatically exemplified in our findings on the "family integration scale," which included such items as the following: "People in our family trust one another"; "My parents know what I am really like as a person"; "I enjoy family life." The hypothesis was that adopted children would feel less integrated than children born into the families. But the scores reported by our four groups of respondents (black TRAs, other TRAs, white born, and white adopted) showed no significant differences; and indeed, among the three largest categories (not including the white adoptees), the mean scores measuring family integration were practically identical: 15.4, 15.2, and 15.4.

Shireman and associates had the TRAs and IRAs rate their parents' behavior toward them in terms of acceptance, rejection, and individuation. They, too, found no significant differences between the mean scores of the two groups, and the majority of the adoptees reported getting along well with both of their parents.

Thus, both sets of our responses—those obtained in 1977 and in 1983–84—consistently portrayed a lack of difference between black and white children in these multiracial families, when differences have been and continue to be present between black and white children reared in the usual single-race family. We concluded after the 1983–84 study that something special seems to happen to both black and white children when they are reared together as siblings in the same family.

In each of the earlier volumes, we also observed—and we believe it is worth repeating here—how impressed we were with the candor and honesty that both the parents and the children displayed in describing their feelings, their hopes, their disappointments, and their regrets during the course of the interviews. At no time during the interviews did this come through more clearly than in the families' evaluations of the quality of their relationships with each other, and in their assessments of the relationships among other members of the family. In their responses to our request to characterize their relationship with each child on a scale of 1 to 4—"basically positive and good" to "basically negative and bad"—the mothers and fathers talked out their feelings, evaluated the pros and cons of their relationships, compared the past few years to the present, and then came up with an answer. In most instances, when the mother and father were participating in the interview together, they provided a joint evaluation—but not always. There were families in which the mothers and fathers disagreed. There was no consistent pattern that associated more negative evaluations to one parent as opposed to the other. When the parents disagreed, however, it was never by more than one position on the scale.

The parents went through the same detailed analyses when they were asked to evaluate the quality of the relationships among their children. The majority were willing to explore their children's personalities, strengths, and weaknesses in great detail.

On the whole, the evaluations were positive, but there were more 2s (i.e., there are problems, but the positive elements outweigh the negative ones) than 1s (i.e., the relationship is basically positive and good). There was no consistent pattern in the parents' evaluation of the birth children as opposed to the children they adopted, nor in their judgments about the relationships between siblings born into the family and those adopted. The parents emphasized "interests," "tastes," "age differences," "jealousy," "competitiveness." The adoptive status of the child was not a prime determinant of those qualities or feelings, according to the parents.

In many families, the children made more positive evaluations about the quality of their family relationships than the parents did. The parents, in some instances, seemed willing to step back and disengage themselves from the situation. The children—and here we have to take special note of the TRAs—continually said, "They are my parents. Yeah, we've had our differences, but I know I can count on them; and I want to be close." This is not meant to indicate that many of the older ones (those in their late teens) were not anxious and ready to move out of the parental home. They were. But the TRAs unequivocally did not perceive their relationships with their parents as temporary or transitory. Practically none of them—even those who expressed anger and bitterness about their current relations—said that they were likely to cut off ties completely or walk out of the family.

Turning to the matter of perceptions about race and racial identities, we reported that 71 percent of the transracial adoptees said they had no problem with the fact that they were the only black or Korean or Native American person in the family. They simply took it for granted. And the same percentages of TRAs as white children answered no to the item that asked, "Have there been times in your life when you wished you were another color?" We did find, however, that, when we asked the children to identify themselves so that someone whom they had never met would recognize them at a meeting place, many more of the TRAs than the white children mentioned race. Such a choice, though, may have more to do with the practicalities of the situation than with any sense of affect or evaluation. If one is black or Korean or Native American in a largely white area, recognition is much easier.

Eleven percent of the TRAs told us directly that they would prefer to be white, and 27 percent of the parents believed that their TRAs identified themselves as white. According to the parents, all of those children were of mixed backgrounds. Since the parents' responses on such matters as their children's choice of friends, dates, interests, aspirations, and the like had demonstrated that they were knowledgeable about and understood their children's thoughts, activities, and tastes, the above-mentioned discrepancy between the children and the parents concerning the former's racial identity should not be assumed to represent the parents' lack of insight or recognition regarding their children's beliefs and desires. But some part of those 27 percent of parents who believed that their TRAs identified themselves as white could reflect wish fulfillment on the part of the parents. Most of those children looked as if they were white; the parents might have liked to believe that the children also considered themselves to be white, like the rest of the family.

Some evidence for this hypothesis came through in the parents' and adolescents' estimates about the adolescents' future. For example, a greater number of TRAs said that they would opt to live in a racially mixed community than did the parents, more of whom thought the TRAs would choose to live in a community like the one in which they were reared (predominantly white). Interestingly, about 25 percent of both the parents and the children thought the children would marry exogamously.

Thus, the evidence we have for parental ambivalence about having a child of a different race is the 16-percent difference between the parents' and adolescents' responses on the item about racial identity, together with the expectations on the part of more TRAs than parents that the former would live in racially mixed rather than predominantly white communities. Neither of these issues, however, is directly tied to the sense of integration or cohesion felt by the parents and the children vis-à-vis their own relationships.

We found that parents and children saw eye to eye on two other race-related issues. First, we reported that 60 percent of the parents and 65 percent of the adolescents told us they talked about race—including racial differences, racial attitudes, and racial discrimination—in their homes. Both parents and adolescents also agreed that the context for most of the discussions involved the families' and children's friends, activities at school, and community events. The next most often cited context concerned political figures, with Jesse Jackson most frequently mentioned. (Remember that many of the interviews were conducted during the 1984 presidential primary campaign.) The third most popular context involved stories on TV and in the newspapers. The birth children were more likely to report discussions of race than were the TRAs.

Second, there was strong agreement between the parents and the children concerning the extent to which the TRAs encountered nasty or unpleasant experiences because of their race. Sixty-five percent of the parents and 67 percent of the TRAs reported at least one such incident. Both the parents and their children agreed that most of these occurrences involved name calling: "nigger," "jungle bunny," "chink," "gook," and so forth. About 10 percent in both groups described incidents in which, in the opinion of the children and the parents, a teacher or the parent of a friend made insulting racist remarks. The majority of the adolescents did not seem to be deeply affected by their encounters; temporary anger—more than hurt—was their main reaction. The parents reported talking to the child about the experience, and in some instances going to the school or talking with the friend's parents. The adoptive parents typically used the experience to make the point that "this is the way of the world" and that the children were likely to encounter even worse situations as they grew older and moved out on their own.

It is interesting to note that, in the Shireman and associates study,

only three of the 35 TRAs reported that they frequently experienced racial incidents in their schools. More than half of the TRAs and almost all of the IRAs said they *never* experienced such incidents. Parents, particularly TRA parents, believed their children had more experiences than the children themselves reported. Only one-third of the teens experiencing racial incidents talked to their parents about them.[8]

We believe that one of the important measures of the parents' unselfish love and concern about their adopted children may be found in their responses to the question about the birth parents. Approximately 40 percent of the parents told us that their children expressed interest in learning about their birth parents. Of those, 7 percent also wanted to locate and meet one or both of their birth parents. An additional 10 percent of the parents had already provided their adopted children with whatever information they had—even prior to, or in the absence of, the children's request. Out of the 40 percent whose children asked about their birth parents, only three parents were sufficiently threatened by the child's interest to refuse to provide the information they had.

As to the matter of "principle," 84 percent of the parents told us that they believed adoptees should have all the information available on their birth records when they are adults. The types of information that some of the parents would withhold included the child's having been born out of wedlock, one or both parents' serving time in prison, or the mother's being a prostitute. Three percent of the parents believed that adoption records should remain closed. An additional 8 percent would place some conditions on opening such records, such as medical need. But the large majority of the parents believed that their adopted child should have access to as much information about her or his birth parents as they could provide, and they do not feel that it was a sign of disloyalty or lack of commitment to them if the child wanted such information.

Looking at the issue from the adoptees' perspective, we found that 38 percent of the TRAs had already tried or were planning to try to locate their birth parents. The others said that they had not decided or did not plan to try to find them. The most typical response was this one: "I am happy with my family. My other parents gave me up." Most of the adoptees did not have deeply rooted feelings about their reasons for wanting to locate their birth parents; curiosity seemed to characterize most of their feelings. Many said, "I would like to see what I will look like when I'm older." Those for whom the issue was more traumatic were children who were adopted when they were three or more years of age, had some memory of a mother, and felt a sense of abandonment or betrayal. They expressed their feelings in this rather muted phrase: "I'll feel incomplete until I do."

It is interesting to note that, in the Shireman and associates study, more of the IRAs (53 percent) than the TRAs (38 percent) not only wanted information about their birth parents, but also expressed interest in meeting them.

Almost three-fourths of the adoptive parents said they were comfortable with their child's meeting their birth parents and would even help them find them. The adoptees have a different perception of this, however. Only 25 percent believe their parents would be comfortable with their meeting their birth parents.[9]

The Fourth Phase

The Parents' Reactions

In the 1990–91 study, we began the parents' interview by asking, "Thinking back, and with the knowledge of hindsight and the experiences you have accumulated, would you have done what you did—adopt a child of a different race?" Ninety-two percent of the parents answered yes; 4 percent said they were not sure; and 4 percent said no. Of the families who said no (i.e., they would not have adopted a nonwhite child), two of the three explained that the child they adopted had preexisting physical and emotional problems they were not aware of at the time of adoption and that those problems had made their lives very difficult. Race was not an issue. The other family simply said that in general it was not a successful experience.

Among the families who said they were not sure, one parent described problems in his marriage and believed they were a factor. In another family the child was afflicted with PKU—a situation that we described in detail in our earlier study reports. The third family believed that in-racial adoption would have been the better choice for the child. The answers are consistent with those we obtained on the three earlier surveys when we asked the parents the same question. Each time, at least 85 percent said yes, they would do it again.

We then asked, "With all of the thought and preparation that had gone into your decision to adopt, what was it about the experience that surprised you the most?" The two most frequently offered answers— made by 22 and 21 percent of the parents, respectively—were that "there have been no major surprises," and that the surprise was how easy or how successful the experience had been. The other two most frequent reactions—each offered by 16 percent of the respondents— were how little information they had been given about their child's physical, emotional, and social backgrounds; and how complicated the teen years were—particularly how their child grappled with identity issues. Other surprises mentioned by at least three families included the following: "how easily our friends and family accepted our TRA children"; "the resistance or disapproval we encountered from our relatives and friends"; "the negative reactions our children received from peers of their own race"; and "the position taken by the National Association of Black Social Workers."

Sixty-eight percent of the parents told us that, in essence, the major impact that parenting a child of a different race had on their lives was that "it broadened and enriched our lives," "it made us more sensitive to racial issues," and "it exposed us to a different culture" and "to different groups that we would not have known or known as well had we not adopted our son" (or daughter).

Finally, we asked the parents—just as we had asked them twenty and eight years earlier—"Would you recommend that other families like your own adopt a child of a different race?" Eighty percent answered yes; 3 percent said no, and 17 percent were not sure. Twenty years earlier, 90 percent said they would recommend TRA to other families; and eight years earlier, 85 percent said they would. Vroegh of Shireman and associates reports after 17 years that 90 percent of the TRA parents and 78 percent of the IRA parents thought transracial adoption was a good idea, with or without provision: "The provision almost always involved parental sensitivity to the needs of the child. Race and color were not an issue."[10]

In our current survey, the reasons given by those families who said they would recommend others to adopt remained unchanged over the 20-year time span. They said in 1991—as they had said in 1972—"Do it because you want a child and because you believe you will love that child as if you had given birth to it"; "Don't do it to show how 'liberal' or 'enlightened' you are," and "Don't listen to what other people say—do what you feel you want to"; "Ask yourself if caring for a child is the most important thing"; "Doing it to have some special status is not a reason to do it."

Among the families who answered they were not sure whether they would recommend TRA to others, most were simply reluctant to give advice on such an important and personal decision, as a matter of principle. One mother said, "Anyone who does it has to have a strong commitment and responsibility to that child. I know too many families who either went the route of giving their child an African name and following all the customs, or of ignoring race completely. You have to have a healthy balance." Another parent said, "The real issue is adoption, not transracial adoption." Others said, "It has to do with how you feel about raising a child that is not biologically your own. If you see it as second rate or second best, it will not work. Race is secondary to your general attitude about adoption"; and, "It would need to be something that a family would embrace as a real encounter, a real mission, a family choice, a family direction in which to go. Never do it out of no other alternative to increasing the size of your family."

The bottom line, then—insofar as the parents are concerned—is that they still stand by their decision of 20 years ago: adopting a child of a different race is a good thing to do. The major impact that the transracial adoption had on their lives was that it broadened and enriched them, exposed them to a different culture, and made them more sensitive to racial issues. Twenty years later, 80 percent would recommend that other families adopt transracially. Most of the other 20 percent were reluctant to offer advice as a matter of principle.

Two families would not recommend adopting across racial lines. Even though the parents in one of the two families said they were glad that *they* did it "because their child would never have had a home," they recommended against it because "it's very wrong to take a child out of his culture unless there's absolutely no other way that the child can be raised by a family." The parents in the other family would not have done it given the knowledge they now had because, in the mother's words, "These kids [a son and a daughter] came from alcoholic families. It was like a cracked plate: it will always be a cracked plate." On the matter of recommending transracial adoption to other families, she offered this advice, "If you do it, have a firm background on their parents."

The Children's Reactions

We were less successful in contacting the children than we were the parents. In 1983, we interviewed 218 children (111 TRAs, 91 birth, and 16 white adoptees). In 1990, we were able to contact and interview 98 children—of whom 55 had been transracially adopted, 30 were birth children, and 13 were white adoptees. We did not try to contact all of the birth children because we thought it more important to interview as many of the adopted—especially the transracially adopted—children as we could locate. While most of the parents stayed put, the children seemed to have been particularly mobile during the period between 1983 and 1990. In large measure, of course, this was a function of their age and status. The median age of the TRAs was 22, and the birth children 26. The median age for the white adoptees was 25. Eighty-five percent of the TRAs and more than 90 percent of the birth children were not living in their parents' home. Locating them (with addresses and/or phone numbers in almost every one of the 50 states, plus some in the armed services and some living abroad) and arranging for personal interviews was extremely time-consuming and expensive. Thus, the fourth phase consisted of 41 black TRAs, 14 other TRAs— almost all of whom were Korean adoptees—13 white adoptees, and 30 birth children.

In 1983, we had asked the respondents to identify by race their three closest friends; 73 percent of the TRAs reported that their closest friend was white, and 71 and 62 percent said their second and third closest friends were white. Among the birth children, 89, 80, and 72 percent said their first, second, and third closest friends were white. In 1990, 53 percent of the TRAs said their closest friend was white, and 70 percent said their second and third closest friends were white. For the birth children, more than 90 percent said their three closest friends were white. Comparison of the two sets of responses—those reported in 1983 and those given in 1990—show that the TRAs had shifted their close friendships from white to nonwhite and a higher percentage of the birth respondents had moved into a white world.

The next portion of the interview focused on a comparison of the respondents' perceptions of their relationship with their parents at the present time and when they were living at home during adolescence; on their reactions to their childhoods; and—for the TRAs—on how they felt about growing up in a white family.

Respondents' answers to the following questions are shown in Chart 5.1: "When you were an adolescent—and at the present time—how would you describe your relationship with your mother—and with your father?" The data indicate that, for the adopted as well as the birth children, relations with both parents improved between adolescence and young adulthood. During adolescence, the TRAs had a more distant relationship with their mothers and fathers than did the birth children; but in the young adult years, more than 80 percent of both

Chart 5.1

How would you describe your relationship with your mother* during adolescence and at the present time?

Quality of Relationship	TRA Adol./Present		White Adopted Adol./Present		Birth Adol./Present	
Very close	29.1	45.5	—	61.5	43.3	50.0
Fairly close	32.7	43.6	53.8	15.4	33.3	30.0
Quite distant	14.5	1.8	23.0	23.0	6.7	6.7
Distant	23.6	5.5	23.0	—	16.7	6.7
No answer	—	3.6	—	—	—	13.3
		N = 55		*N* = 13		*N* = 30

How would you describe your relationship with your father* during adolescence and at the present time?

Quality of Relationship	TRA Adol./Present		White Adopted Adol./Present		Birth Adol./Present	
Very close	30.9	43.6	7.7	38.5	43.3	36.7
Fairly close	34.5	38.2	61.5	53.8	30.0	43.3
Quite distant	14.5	3.6	15.4	7.7	3.3	6.7
Distant	18.2	10.9	15.4	—	20.0	10.0
No answer	1.8	3.6	—	—	3.3	3.3

*For the adopted children, the term *adopted* mother and father was included in the question.

the TRAs and the birth children described their relationship to their mothers and their fathers as very or fairly close.

In 1983, we asked the TRAs and the birth children this question: "Looking ahead to a time when you will not be living in your parents' house, do you expect that you will feel close to them (e.g., discuss things that are bothering you or that you consider important)?" We divided the respondents by sex as well as adopted status and found that there were no real differences by either category, as shown in Chart 5.2.

The respondents' ties to their siblings during adolescence, and currently, is shown in Chart 5.3. Not as dramatically as in their relationship with their parents—but in the same direction—the respondents' relationship with an older or only sibling improved over time. For both the birth and the adopted children, a higher proportion reported that they had closer ties with that sibling at the present time than when they were adolescents. The pattern showing closer ties in the present with the second sibling holds for the birth children but not for the TRAs, although the large majority of respondents in both categories report close relationships with both their first and second siblings.

We asked the TRAs a series of questions about their relationships to family members during their childhood and adolescence, many of which focused on racial differences. The first such question was this: "Do you remember when you first realized that you looked different from your parents?" to which 75 percent answered that they did not remember. The others mentioned events such as "at family gatherings," "when my parents first came to school," "on vacations," or "when we were doing out-of-the-ordinary activities," and "immediately, at the time of adoption." The latter response was made by children who were not infants at the time of their adoption.

Chart 5.2

Looking ahead to a time when you will not be living in your parents' house, do you expect that you will feel close to them?

	Mean Scores	
	TRA	*Birth*
Males	2.2	2.2
Females	2.5	2.2

1 = very close; 2 = close; 3 = fairly close; 4 = not at all close

Chart 5.3

How would you describe your relationship with your (specific sibling, e.g., older, younger, brother or sister specified) during adolescence and at the present time?

Sibling #1

Quality of Relationship	TRA Adol./Present		White Adopted Adol./Present		Birth Adol./Present	
Very close	27.3	30.9	7.7	38.5	46.7	43.3
Fairly close	30.9	43.6	69.2	38.5	36.7	43.3
Quite distant	18.2	10.9	—	—	10.0	3.3
Distant	20.0	12.7	15.4	15.4	6.7	10.0
Not app./No answer	3.6	1.8	7.7	7.7	—	—

Sibling #2

Quality of Relationship	TRA* Adol./Present		White Adopted Adol./Present		Birth* Adol./Present	
			(*N*s are too small)			
Very close	25.0	20.9			20.0	30.0
Fairly close	45.4	48.8			46.7	46.7
Quite distant	15.9	9.3			20.0	13.3
Distant	13.6	20.9			13.3	10.0

*Based on the 43 respondents who reported having a second sibling.

That question was followed by this one: "How do you think the fact that you had a different racial background from your birth brother(s) and/or sister(s) affected your relationship with them as you were growing up?" Almost 90 percent of those who had siblings said it made little or no difference. The few others were divided among those who said that it had a positive effect, or a negative effect, or that they were not sure what, if any, effect it had.

We continued with this question: "Was being of a different race from your adoptive family easier or harder during various stages of your life?" Forty percent responded that they rarely found it difficult; 24 percent said the teen years were the most difficult; 22 percent found early childhood the most difficult; 8 percent said they found early childhood the easiest; and another 8 percent said they had a difficult time throughout their childhood and adolescence. Twenty-nine percent said that people of the same racial background as their own reacted "very negatively" or "negatively" toward them during their adolescence. The other responses ranged from "neutral" (37 percent) to "positive" (10 percent) and "very positive" (15 percent).

We asked the birth children how they felt about living in a family with black or other nonwhite siblings. Only one respondent reported "somewhat negative" feelings about having a sibling of a different race, and this same respondent felt his parents had made a mistake in their decision to adopt a black child. Thirty percent acknowledged that there were times during their childhood when they felt out of place in their families—for example, when their families participated in "ethnic ceremonies" or attended black churches. But when asked, "How do you think being white by birth but having nonwhite siblings affected how you perceive yourself today?" all but 13 percent answered that the experience "had no effect." The others cited positive affects such as "it broadened my understanding" and it "made me think of myself as part of the human race rather than of any special racial category."

Among those children whose parents lived in the same community, all of the TRAs and the birth children said they saw their parents at least two or three times a month; most saw them almost every day or a couple of times a week.

On the 1983 survey, we asked the children a modified version of the following question: "If you had a serious personal problem (involving your marriage, your children, your health, etc.), who is the first person you would turn to; who is the next; who is the third?" Two other problems were posed: "money," and "if you were in trouble with the law." In 1983, 46.8 percent of the TRAs chose a parent or a sibling; 45 percent of the birth children chose a parent or sibling; and 25 percent of the white adoptees chose a parent or a sibling.

In 1990—seven years later—when we again asked the children, "If you had a serious personal problem . . .", we found no evidence that the TRAs were less integrated into their families than were the birth children. As shown in Charts 5.4, 5.5, and 5.6, the TRAs were as likely or more likely, to turn to parents and siblings as were the birth or white adopted children. But in almost all instances, the first persons that children in all three categories turned to were their adopted or birth parents. For the TRAs, a sibling was the next person. For the birth children, spouses and/or girlfriends or boyfriends constituted the second likely choice. The birth children and the white adoptees were older than the TRAs (median age 26 and 25 vs. 22), and this may

Chart 5.4

Who are the first, second, and third persons you would seek out if you had a serious personal problem?

Persons	TRAs			White Adopted			Birth		
	1st	*2nd*	*3rd*	*1st*	*2nd*	*3rd*	*1st*	*2nd*	*3rd*
Parents	47.3	40.0	36.4	30.8	15.4	23.1	24.6	43.4	33.3
Siblings	9.1	23.6	—	23.1	30.8	7.7	3.3	20.0	13.3
Friends	29.1	27.3	32.7	23.1	30.8	14.4	23.3	26.7	33.3
Spouse/ Boy/girl friends	12.7	5.4	3.6	7.7	7.7	23.1	46.6	3.3	6.7
Other	—	1.8	20.0	7.7	—	15.4	—	3.3	3.3
No answer	1.8	1.8	7.3	7.7	15.4	15.4	3.3	3.3	10.0

explain their lesser likelihood to turn to their parents for help or advice.

Location of birth parents was another issue we raised with the adopted children in the third phase of our study and again in 1990–91. In 1983–84, there were 22.5 percent who said they had tried to locate their birth parents; an additional 15 percent said they would like to try, and 25 percent said they were not sure but they might try, to locate their birth parents sometime in the future. Thirty-seven percent expressed no interest in locating their birth parents. In 1990–91, 75 percent said they had not tried to locate either of their birth parents. Among those who did make the effort, only one tried to locate a birth father; the others sought out their birth mothers. Of the 15 TRAs who tried to locate their birth parents, seven were successful. Of those seven, three characterized their current relationship with their birth mothers as very or fairly close; the other four considered it somewhat or very distant. Thirteen of the 15 asked for and obtained the help of their adopted parents in locating their birth mothers. The other two did not ask their adopted parents for help. Thus, over the years, most of the adopted children opted not to try to locate birth parents. For the small minority who did, it did not turn out to be a wholly positive or special experience.

The last part of the interview focused on finding out how the TRAs felt about the practice of placing nonwhite—especially black—children in white homes, what recommendations they might have about adoption practices, and what advice they might have for white parents who

Chart 5.5

Who are the first, second, and third persons you would seek out if you had a serious money problem?

Persons	TRAs			White Adopted			Birth		
	1st	2nd	3rd	1st	2nd	3rd	1st	2nd	3rd
Parents	70.9	38.2	16.4	84.6	53.8	7.7	56.7	40.0	23.4
Siblings	9.1	14.5	14.5	—	—	7.7	6.7	13.3	10.0
Friends	3.6	9.1	23.6	—	7.7	23.1	3.3	16.7	20.0
Spouse/ Boy/girl friends	7.2	1.8	1.8	7.7	—	15.4	16.7	10.0	3.3
Other	7.2	12.7	7.3	—	15.4	15.4	10.7	6.7	16.6
No answer	1.8	23.6	36.4	7.7	23.1	30.8	6.6	16.7	26.7

are considering transracial adoption. We also asked the respondents to evaluate their own experience with transracial adoption.

We opened the topic by stating, "You have probably heard of the position taken by the National Association of Black Social Workers and several councils of Native Americans strongly opposing transracial adoption. Do you agree or disagree with their position?" All of the respondents were aware of the NABSWs position. Eighty percent of the TRAs and 70 percent of the birth children said they disagreed with the NABSW position. Among the latter, 17 percent agreed and 13 percent were not sure. Only 5 percent of the TRAs agreed with the NABSW's position; the others were not sure how they felt about the issue. The reasons most often given for why they disagreed were that "racial differences are not crucial," "TRA is the best practical alternative," and "having a loving, secure relationship in a family setting is all important."

One black male adoptee said,

My parents have never been racist. They took shit for adopting two black kids. I'm proud of them for it. The Black Social Workers' Association promotes a separatist ideology.

Another black female commented,

It's a crock—it's just ridiculous. They [the NABSW] should be happy to get families for these children—period. My parents made sure we grew

Chart 5.6

Who are the first, second, and third persons you would seek out if you had trouble with the law?

	TRAs			White Adopted			Birth		
Persons	*1st*	*2nd*	*3rd*	*1st*	*2nd*	*3rd*	*1st*	*2nd*	*3rd*
Parents	58.2	47.3	9.1	53.8	38.5	23.1	33.4	40.0	33.2
Siblings	10.9	14.5	16.4	15.4	15.4	7.7	13.3	26.6	3.3
Friends	7.3	20.0	25.5	—	15.4	15.4	16.7	13.3	33.3
Spouse/ Boy/girl friends	18.2	—	7.3	15.4	7.7	7.7	26.6	10.0	10.0
Other	3.6	9.1	14.5	7.7	—	7.7	6.6	6.6	9.9
No answer	1.8	9.1	27.3	7.7	23.1	38.5	3.3	3.3	10.0

up in a racially diverse neighborhood. Now I am fully comfortable with who I am.

Another commented,

> I feel lucky to have been adopted when I was very young [24 days]. I was brought up to be self-confident—to be the best I can. I was raised in an honest environment.

In response to the question "Would you urge social workers and adoption agencies to place nonwhite children in white homes?" 70 percent of the TRAs and 67 percent of the birth children said yes without qualifications or stipulations. Almost all of the others placed some stipulations, the most common of which was that it should not be the placement of first choice—that a search should be made to find appropriate families of the same racial background as the children. The second most frequently mentioned stipulation was that the children should be placed with those white families who are "willing to make a commitment to exposing the child to his or her native culture."

We then shifted to a more personal note and asked, "How do you think being black (or, where appropriate, Korean or Native American) and raised by white parents has affected how you perceive yourself today?" One-third of the TRAs thought the adoption had a positive effect on their self-image. One-third thought it had no effect, and one-third did not know what effect the adoption had on their self-image.

One male adoptee said, "Multicultural attitudes develop better children. I was brought up without prejudice. The experience is fulfilling and enriching for parents and children.''

Our next question was this: ''All things considered, would you have preferred to have been adopted by parents whose racial background was the same as yours?'' Seven percent said yes; 67 percent said no; 4 percent said they were not sure or did not know; and 22 percent did not answer. When asked why they held the position they did, most said, in essence, ''My life has worked out very well''; ''My parents love me''; and/or ''Race is not that important.''

One female black adoptee believed she ''got the best of both worlds. I can be myself and have black and white friends. I don't look at people for their race.''

Another said, ''The transracial adoption experience gives us an open view of the world. Prejudice comes from ignorance.''

When asked what advice they would give to parents who have the opportunity to adopt a young child of ''your racial background,'' and about how she or he should be reared, 91 percent advised mostly that such parents be sensitive to racial issues; 9 percent advised that they reconsider.

One of the transracial adoptees who agrees with the position of the NABSW said, ''I feel that I missed out on Black culture. I can sit and read a book about Martin Luther King, but it is not the same.'' His advice to white parents who adopt black children is this: ''Make sure they [the TRAs] have the influence of Blacks in their lives; even if you have to go out and make friends with Black families. It's a must—otherwise you are cheating them [the TRAs] of something valuable.''

The last question we asked the TRAs was how they would describe their own racial backgrounds. Among the black TRAs, 32 percent answered black, and 68 percent said they were mixed (mostly black-white, a few black-Asians, and some black–Native Americans). Among the other TRAs, 36 percent described themselves as mixed, and 7 percent as white; the other 57 percent labeled themselves Native American, Korean, and Hispanic.

Notes

1. Rita J. Simon and Howard Altstein, *Transracial Adoption* (New York: John Wiley and Sons, 1977).

2. Rita J. Simon and Howard Altstein, *Adoption, Race, and Identity* (New York, Praeger, 1992).

3. Lucille J. Grow and Deborah Shapiro, *Black Children, White Parents: A Study of Transracial Adoption* (New York: Child Welfare League of America, 1974).

4. Rita J. Simon and Howard Altstein, *Transracial Adoption: A Follow Up* (Lexington, Mass.: Lexington Books, 1981), p. 29.

5. Karen S. Vroegh, "Transracial Adoption: How It Is 17 Years Later," unpublished report, Chicago Child Care Society, Chicago, April 1992, p. 20.

6. Ibid., p. 32.

7. Simon and Altstein, *Transracial Adoption* (1977), p. 147.

8. Vroegh, "Transracial Adoption," p. 33.

9. Ibid., p. 40.

10. Ibid., p. 41.

6

Policy Recommendations

This chapter considers other solutions to the problem of parentless minority children. We start with the premise that adoption (i.e., permanent placement in a family setting) serves a child's interest better than foster care, group homes, or other forms of institutional living. A solution already in practice—but one we urge be given more extensive consideration and support—is subsidized adoption. We especially recommend reexamination of the linkage between foster care and subsidized adoption, with an eye toward both strengthening this connection and increasing its use.

Foster Care and Subsidized Adoption

Although foster care was initially designed to provide temporary, time-limited care for children removed from their families, over the decades an unintended consequence has developed. Children placed in foster care remain there far in excess of what the concept originally intended. The paradoxical term *permanent-temporary placement* has entered the vocabulary of child welfare.

Foster care was originally conceived to be the short-term removal of a child(ren) from their homes while, with the assistance of a social worker, parent(s) dealt with problems requiring their absence. After a "defined and limited" period of time, one or two plans would be put into effect: the child would return home following resolution of the problem(s) requiring her or his removal; or, if return was not possible, another "permanent" plan would be designed. In either case, the child would not remain in foster care, which was designed as a short-term removal of the child from her or his birth family.

What in fact occurs in many cases is that the child remains in foster care for long periods of time, creating a contradictory system of long-term semipermanent placements *without further planning*—a twilight zone that is neither temporary nor permanent. An example of this unintended consequence may be seen in a 1989 report issued by the House of Representatives Select Committee on Children, Youth, and Families. The committee's survey found that in 1985 there were 39 percent of all children in foster care who had been there longer than two years. This figure had not substantially changed since 1983. During this same two-year interval, the overall percentage of children in foster care increased 14 percent.

The irony of the above is that P.L. 96-272 (the Adoption Assistance and Child Welfare Act of 1980)—legislated with great fanfare—was not only designed to reconfigure state child-welfare services in adoption and foster care, but specifically intended to provide the states with financial incentives to reduce the time a child remained in foster care, and to develop programs designed to prevent initial placement into foster care. It also required that a child be placed in the least restrictive setting and that, within 18 months of removal from her or his home, a permanent plan be developed for each child. A permanency plan was authorized to prevent what has come to be called "foster care drift," whereby a child drifted from foster home to foster home until the age of majority and was then discharged into society. The law also called for states to provide subsidies for "special needs" children (e.g., racial and ethnic minorities) when reunification with their birth families was not possible and if they were eligible for Aid for Dependent Children (AFDC) and Supplemental Security Income (SSI).

Even with the above legislation, the decade of the 1980s saw hundreds of thousands of children experiencing foster care, and their numbers continue to climb. The select committee reported that, between 1985 and 1988, the number of children in foster care rose 23 percent (to approximately 340,300) after falling 9 percent between 1980 and 1985. Should the trend continue, the report projected, the number of children in foster care would approach 553,000 by 1995.

In those instances in which adoption was the planned goal, in many cases it was the foster parents who were the social worker's candidates to become adoptive parents. In fact, a 1988 report indicated that 61 percent of all minority adoptions were to foster parents, with a range of 40–80 percent.[1] Additional support for the notion of foster-parent adoptions may be found in practically all state laws and in the federal "Model Adoption Act" and "Model Statute for Termination of Parental Rights." Each of these documents looks to the foster parents as priority targets for adoption of children already in their care. Indeed, many foster parents do intend to become, or want to become, adoptive parents. This seems a reasonable and logical consequence, given the intimacy associated with any type of parenting. That more foster parents do not become adoptive parents is due in not a few instances to a lack of money. Many foster families cannot afford to adopt the child(ren) in their care without the use of subsidies, because in nonsubsidized adoptions all financial payments given to a family in support of a child while she or he is in foster care must stop after the child is adopted.

In a 1975 article, Julian Simon examined foster care data for three years, from 32 states plus the District of Columbia.[2] He found that doubling foster care payments increased the pool of foster families from 50 to 100 percent. It is reasonable to assume that, if increased subsidy payments were made available to potential adopters, there would be an increase in the number of foster parents who would want to adopt.

We recommend that programs continue payments to foster parents after adoption (i.e., subsidized adoption), or use the payments as an incentive to attract adoptive parents. Such payments, we believe, would increase the likelihood that minority foster parents will become adoptive parents.

One of the unexpected—yet not surprising—consequences of foster care is that minority children are significantly overrepresented in its ranks. In 1985, of all children in foster care 41 percent were minorities. By 1988, that figure rose to 46 percent. Minority children also *remain* in foster care one-third longer than white children.

Nonwhite status is one criterion for placement in the special-needs category. The evidence that subsidies to foster parents are a successful method of encouraging adoption is realized when we see that 90 percent of all children adopted with the use of this program were adopted by their foster families. The literature also agrees that subsidies are an effective method of achieving permanent homes (i.e., adoption) for minority children.

In addition to considerable institutional support for subsidized adoption by leading child-welfare organizations (e.g., from the CWLA), the federal government itself developed a "Model State Subsidized Adoption Act" to be used as a prototype by the individual states. One of the act's tenets is its lack of a means test for potential adopters. It emphasizes that the needs of a child for adoption should be paramount, eclipsing the finances of the potential adopter. Not only would adoption achieve permanency and stability for the child(ren) in question; but in the long run, a more liberal use of subsidies might end up costing federal and state governments less money. It clearly would not cost more, since in no case can subsidy payments be greater than the amount the foster parents receive if the child remains in foster care.

One way, then, to reduce the number of nonwhite free-for-adoption children in long-term foster care would be to encourage their foster parents to consider adoption with the use of the above-mentioned subsidies. In fact, P.L. 96-272 supports the idea of subsidized adoption by foster parents when the child appears to have bonded with them. Should adoption by minority foster-care parents prove successful, it would be reasonable to assume that the number of nonwhite children available for adoption by other families would lessen. Reducing this pool would also reduce the "temptation" to consider white families as adopters for these children. Moreover, in support of the idea that there is a potential availability of black families for black children, a recent statistic indicates that one out of every three black families would be interested in adoption.[3]

One of the obstacles to greater use and acceptance of adoption subsidies may be that the concept itself runs counter to our deepest cultural beliefs. The idea that society should pay someone to "become a parent" through adoption—as differentiated from paying one "to parent" through foster care—may be anathema to many people.

Intercountry Adoption

Those in the West who are opposed to intercountry adoption (ICA) argue that conditions need to be changed in the countries allowing their children to be adopted in the West. Rene Hoksbergen, a leading advocate of keeping children in their society of birth, argues,

> The transport of children from distant countries to give them a chance in Western families must be viewed ambivalently: it seems questionable to move children thousands of miles from their ancestors and origins. Let us hope that culture and economic circumstances in all Third World countries change to the extent that it will be the exception when a child's only chance for a satisfactory upbringing exists with a family thousands of miles from its birthplace.[4]

Opponents also argue that Western families who want to adopt should turn their attention to the thousands of available children in their native countries who have special needs because they are emotionally or physically handicapped or are of minority racial backgrounds, are beyond infancy, and/or are sibling group members. It is to these children that couples seeking to adopt should focus their attention, not on healthy foreign-born infants, argue the opponents of ICA.

While recognizing the plight of native-born children, the families who want to adopt healthy foreign-born infants and the organizations that support intercountry adoptions claim that what they are doing is offering such children better lives than they would have if they remained in their birth countries. At the same time, these families are also satisfying their own need to parent an infant. By allowing the child to be adopted by a Western family and live in a more affluent and advantaged society, the child's birth country is offering it a lifetime opportunity. Thus, pro-ICA groups argue, the child is salvaged from poverty and deprivation, and the childless parents realize their dream of raising a child from infancy.

There is probably no single solution that would satisfy the concerns of the various groups involved in the debate over the merits of intercountry adoptions. In summary, three complex conditions are interwoven:

1. Large numbers of legally adoptable children exist within Western countries (particularly the United States), many of whom will spend their entire childhoods in temporary placements (foster care, group homes, etc.), awaiting adoption.

2. Even larger numbers of couples exist who want to adopt a child and would like that child to be an infant.

3. Thousands of seemingly orphaned, healthy children—many of whom are infants—exist in developing countries, with little chance of in-country adoption.

To complicate the issue even more, another factor has emerged in the past few years, namely, the declining numbers of healthy foreign-born infants who are available for adoption in the West. As we noted in Chapter 1, Korea—historically the largest supplier of children to Western families—has dramatically decreased the number of children it is willing to allow to leave the country, and there is considerable speculation that it will reduce this practice even further in the near future. Other countries will probably follow Korea's example, thereby reducing the overall availability of foreign-born children for adoption in the West. The children in the countries that continue to allow foreign adoptions will be at a premium, thereby increasing competition for them and raising the costs involved.

Western couples will thus have little recourse but to explore other possibilities for obtaining a child. Such possibilities could include an increased interest in the many forms of medical technology now available in the "fertility" area (in-vitro techniques, sperm and egg banks, etc.), more emphasis on private adoptions, perhaps another look at surrogacy, and hopefully a willingness to reexamine adopting children other than infants. Should the latter occur—especially with subsidy incentives, as mentioned earlier—some of the many thousands of adoptable American children would be given opportunities heretofore reserved for foreign-born infants. This can only occur on a meaningful scale if the forces opposed to interracial placements relax their opposition. Unless this opposition is reduced, agencies and individual social workers will continue to be reluctant to sanction transracial adoptions; and in the absence of any large-scale recruitment of nonwhite families willing to adopt, many children will be consigned to permanent-temporary placements in foster homes, or will live out their childhood in institutions.

Notes

1. *Minority Adoptions,* report issued by the Office of the Inspector General, Office of Analysis and Inspection, July 1988, pp. 9 and 11; also found in "The Resource File," *Roundtable,* no. 1 (1992), p. 8.

2. Julian L. Simon, "The Effect of Foster-care Payment Levels on the Number of Foster Children Given Homes," *Social Service Review* (September 1975), p. 405.

3. "Resource File," p. 14.

4. Rene Hoksbergen, "Intercountry Adoption Coming of Age in the Netherlands," in Howard Altstein and Rita J. Simon, eds., *Intercountry Adoption* (New York: Praeger, 1991), p. 156.

7

Concluding Remarks

This volume marks the end of our 20-year study of transracial adoptees and their families. We began our study in the fall of 1971 by interviewing parents and their children (adopted and birth) who were between four and seven years old, and conducted the last set of interviews with the adult children (adopted and birth) in 1991. We surveyed the families four times—in 1971–72, 1979, 1983, and 1991. In between, there were occasional contacts with some of the families, often in response to a request from the print or electronic media for interviews. Rita Simon would call and ask if any family members were interested.

The major findings from our 20-year saga have been reported and discussed in this volume and in our earlier ones.[1] At each phase of the study, we reported the problems, setbacks, and disappointments, as well as the successes, joys, and optimism about the future. None of the families disrupted the adoption. There were separations and family breakups as a result of parental deaths and divorces. During the pre-adolescent years when the adoptees were 11 or 12 years old, we reported that, in about 20 percent of the families, the adoptees were stealing from other family members. The children stole money from their mother's purse, and phonographs, bikes, and skates from their siblings. Most often they gave the items away. They did not try to sell them, and the adoptees did not engage in other delinquent acts. Were these behaviors a function of the children's adopted status, their racial differences, or a combination of both? How long was this likely to continue, and would the children be likely to engage in other forms of delinquent and criminal behavior as they grew older? We could find no references to these behaviors in previous studies that had been done with adopted children; but when we sought out clinicians whose caseloads often involved adoptees, we were told that intrafamily stealing was not unusual. It was the adopted children's form of testing.

How much of a commitment did their families have toward them? Were the families prepared to keep them when things got rough, when they did not behave like model children? Were they really a part of the family, for better or worse?

Four years later when we studied the families for the third time, none of them reported that the stealing had continued. It just stopped. But, as we discovered in the course of our interviews with the parents and the adolescents, all was not sweetness and light during the years of adolescence. Families reported drinking and drug problems; there were some runaways and truants, as well as mothers and fathers divorced. But we also found that there were no differences between the birth children and the adopted children in the likelihood of problems occurring. The activities ran in families; they were not favored by either the adoptees or the birth children; and race was not a salient characteristic.

In the last phase—when most of the respondents were no longer living with their parents—the adoptees were as much in touch with their parents, and felt as much a part of their families, as did the birth children. Earlier, during the adolescent years, the scores on the self-esteem and family-integration scales had shown no difference between the transracial adoptees and the birth children.

On the matter of racial identity and racial awareness, we had reported 20 years earlier that both the black and the white children—the transracial adoptees and the birth children—selected "black," "white," and "in-between" dolls at random. Unlike all other previous doll studies, our respondents did not favor the white doll. It was not considered smarter, prettier, nicer, and so forth, than the black doll by either the white or the black children. Neither did the other projective tests conducted during the same time period reveal preferences for white, or negative reactions to black. Yet the black and white children in our study accurately identified themselves as white or black on those same tests.

Over the years, we continued to ask about and measure racial attitudes, racial awareness, and racial identity among the adopted and birth children. We also questioned the parents—during the first three phases of the study—about the activities, if any, that they as a family engaged in to enhance their transracial adoptee's racial awareness and identity. We reported them having conversations about race and racial issues over dinner, watching the TV series *Roots*, joining black churches, seeking out black godparents, preparing Korean food, traveling to Native American festivals, and having lots of books, artifacts, and music about blacks, Koreans, Native Americans, and other cultures. As the years progressed, we found that the children—rather than the parents—were more likely to want to call a halt to these types of activities. "Not every dinner conversation has to be a lesson in black history," and "We are more interested in basketball and football than in ceremonial dances," were the comments we heard frequently from the TRAs as they were growing up.

But we found that, both during adolescence and later as adults, the TRAs clearly were aware of and comfortable with their racial identity. They both laughed at and were somewhat scornful of the NABSW's characterization of them as "oreos—black on the outside, white on the inside." As young adults, the black adoptees stressed their comfort with their black identity and their awareness that they may speak, dress, and have different tastes in music than inner-city blacks—but that the black experience is a varied one in this society, and they are no less black than are children of the ghetto.

Throughout the study, we also described how the birth children were reacting to the transracial adoption experience. In the early years, we reported occasional expressions of annoyance and anger at how much time and energy their parents were devoting to their adopted sibling: "Our family life has been turned upside down since 'D' came home," or 'M' gets all the attention." But these remarks were few and far between. In the large majority of the families, the black adoptee was "my brother" or "my sister"—to be cared about, played with, and, if necessary, protected. Race receded into the background. When fights and conflicts occurred, they were a function of personality, age, and gender differences. Both the parents and the children described the problems as "typical sibling rivalry." As adults, the birth children now talk about the special window they had during childhood, from which they were able to observe how blacks and whites interact with each other and how families and communities respond to racial differences. They feel that their lives were enriched by the transracial adoption experience, and that they—like their black brother or Korean sister— have entered a more complex social world than would have been available to them had they grown up in an all-white family.

Having reported a basically positive outcome for our 20-year study, and having been able to show the baselessness of the warnings and fears of the NABSW that the TRAs would grow up confused and ambivalent about their racial identities and "unable to cope with the racism that is endemic in American society," it would be wonderful to be also able to report that policies have changed and that transracial adoptions have become accepted and widespread. Unfortunately, the latter has not happened, and there are no signs that the NABSW has softened or changed its stand against transracial adoption. Even as thousands of black children continue to spend years in institutions and in foster care, the NABSW continues to adhere to its 1971 position: that institutionalization and foster care are better than transracial adoption. One can only continue to wonder—better for whom? Certainly for those of us who support the courts' standard of seeking to serve the "best interest of the child," adoption—permanent placement in a family—has to be a better solution. And because we believe that adoption serves the best interest of the child, we also urge the continued and expanded use of subsidies to encourage and allow more families to adopt, especially because many of the potential parents in these families are likely to be foster parents of minority ethnic backgrounds.

Public opinion data show that a majority of the American public, black and white, supports transracial adoptions over institutional living or foster care. At its annual convention in July 1992, the membership of the NAACP passed a resolution that stated, "If black families are not available for placement of black children, transracial adoption ought to be pursued as a viable and preferable alternative to keeping children in foster homes."[2]

The law condemns the use of race as the sole basis for an adoption decision, and allows its consideration only as a factor in determining the best interest of the child. Therefore, it is a mark of the low visibility of much of the adoption process that the racial objectives promoted by the NABSW can be as influential as they have been.

Three states have statutes that mandate racial matching; about ten other states have administrative policies with the same requirement. None of these statutes or policies have been upheld. In at least two cases, they have been struck down as unconstitutional.

Hopefully, more legal challenges to mandatory racial matching policies will be brought, so that the illegality of the process will become more widely publicized.

We end this volume—and our 20-year study—with a plea. Move the thousands of children who are available for adoption out of the institutions and out of their temporary foster placements, and into permanent homes! Apply the standard *best interest of the child* as the first and foremost criterion in child placement! Make the move without regard to race!

Notes

1. Rita J. Simon and Howard Altstein, *Transracial Adoption* (New York: John Wiley and Sons, 1977); *Transracial Adoption: A Follow Up* (Lexington, Mass.: Lexington Books, 1981); *Transracial Adoptees and Their Families* (New York: Praeger, 1987); *Identity* (New York: Praeger, 1992).

2. National Association for the Advancement of Colored People, resolution of the Annual National Convention, Nashville, Tenn., 1992.

Index

Abortion, 1, 13–14

Adolescents: adoption and, 35, 51, 57, 58, 60, 87, 91, 97, 114

Adopted children: age of, 26, 53, 56, 57, 60, 62–63, 66, 67, 68, 81, 82, 98; best interests of, 21, 24, 35, 48, 51, 52, 116; gender of, 59, 61, 80–81; problems of, 51, 57, 63, 64, 65, 67, 72–73, 86, 93–94, 113–14; relationships with adoptive families, 15, 53, 73, 75, 78–79, 86, 89–90, 97–101, 114–15; rights of, 27, 42–43. *See also* Adolescents; Infants; Parentless children

Adopting Older Kids, 45

Adoption: barriers to, 4–5, 27, 31; cost of, 10–11, 27, 109, 112; disruption of, 59, 113; policies toward, 2, 21–22, 27–28, 48–49, 116; rates of, 5, 7, 8, 11–14, 22, 44; same-race, 5, 17, 22, 54, 56–57, 94. *See also* Adoption agencies; Adoption laws; Adoptive parents; Intercountry adoption; Transracial adoption

Adoption agencies, 21–23, 47, 56, 67, 80, 103; private, 1, 5, 15–16, 17, 27; public, 15–16, 31, 45; race and placement by, 5, 7, 43–44, 48, 49, 80. *See also* Child welfare agencies

Adoption Assistance and Child Welfare Act of 1980, 2–3, 20, 46, 108, 110

Adoption laws, 2, 15–29, 108, 116; constitutional issues in, 17–19; international, 27–32, 67. *See also* Adoption Assistance and Child Welfare Act of 1980; Indian Child Welfare Act of 1978

Adoptive parents, 1, 5, 15–16, 27, 34, 48; availability of, 5, 42, 48, 49, 80, 110, 116; black, 5, 10, 21, 40, 42, 43, 44, 48, 49, 80, 110, 116; motivations of, 39, 42, 53, 68, 77–82, 95, 109; prospective, 21, 22, 108–109, 112; socioeconomic status of, 10–11, 27, 44, 46, 56, 61, 75–77, 83–84, 111; suitability of, 4–5, 11–14, 15, 16, 27–28, 31, 45, 46, 109–110; waiting by, 5, 6–7, 11, 27, 31; white, 3, 5, 10, 4–43, 53–54, 71, 77–82. *See also* Adopted children; Racism

African American Child Welfare Act, proposed, 49

African American children. *See* Black children

Altstein, Howard, 44, 51, 62, 63. *See also* Simon-Altstein 20-year study

American Indian Policy Review Commission, 20

Arizona, 6, 18, 33–35